Infographics Powered by SAS®

Data Visualization Techniques for Business Reporting

Travis Murphy

sas.com/books

The correct bibliographic citation for this manual is as follows: Travis Murphy. 2018. *Infographics Powered by SAS®: Data Visualization Techniques for Business Reporting*. Cary, NC: SAS Institute Inc.

Infographics Powered by SAS®: Data Visualization Techniques for Business Reporting

Copyright © 2018, SAS Institute Inc., Cary, NC, USA

ISBN 978-1-63526-280-3 (Hard copy)
ISBN 978-1-63526-356-5 (EPUB)
ISBN 978-1-63526-357-2 (MOBI)
ISBN 978-1-63526-358-9 (PDF)

Contents

About This Book

What does this book cover?

A picture is worth a thousand words, but what if there are a billion words? This is where the picture becomes even more important, and this is where infographics step in. Infographics are a representation of information in a graphic format designed to make the data easily understandable, at a glance, without having to have a deep knowledge of the data. Because of the amount of data available today, more business infographics are being created to communicate the information and insight from all available data, both in the boardroom and on social media. This book shows you how to create information graphics that can be printed, shared, and dynamically explored with objects and data from SAS® Visual Analytics. Connect your business infographics to the high-performance analytical engine from SAS® for repeatability, scale, and performance on big data and for ease of use.

You learn how to leverage elements of your corporate dashboards and self-service analytics while communicating subjective information and adding the context that business teams require, in a highly visual format. This book looks at how SAS® Office Analytics enables a Microsoft Office user to create business infographics for all occasions. You will learn a workflow that lets you get the most from your SAS system without having to code anything, unless you want to code, and then this book has something for you also. This book combines the perfect blend of creative freedom and data governance that comes from leveraging the power of SAS and the familiarity of Microsoft Office.

Topics covered in this book include:

- SAS Visual Analytics
- SAS/Graph® (SAS Code Examples)
- Data Visualization with SAS
- Create reports with SAS
- Use reports and graphs from SAS to create business presentations
- Use SAS within Microsoft Office

Is This Book for You?

This book is for all SAS users.

If the reader is an intermediate or advanced SAS user than this book will assist them in understanding the value of information graphics and the possibilities they provide them and engaging their audience.

For a beginner SAS user this book provides the necessary overview to understand information graphics foundations and origins to then progress through the book and use the step by step examples to work along with.

This book is aimed at SAS users who create and design reports and dashboards for their users. Managers can use this book to determine what their teams could create and design with SAS Visual Analytics and SAS® Office Analytics.

All levels of SAS skills are covered in this book: beginners, intermediate and advanced. The beginner learns to use SAS Add-in for Microsoft office, intermediate user gets to extend the office examples, and use SAS Visual Analytics to go a step further, and the advanced user gets to see the power of the SAS code base to achieve this common business goal: the infographic.

Prerequisites

You do not have to have any previous experience with SAS tools to read this book. However, if you do have some experience with SAS code and data preparation, then you may find some parts of this book and examples easier.

Examples: Data, Reports and Code

There are examples provided in this book including code samples, reports and data. These files can be downloaded and are available at the following location:

http://support.sas.com/murphy

Software used

Support Documentation at http://support.sas.com/documentation/

Here are the specific software versions used in this book:

- Microsoft Office 2016
- SAS Visual Analytics 8.2
- SAS Office Analytics 9.4 M5
- SAS Add-In for Microsoft Office 7.15

Documentation links and further reading are outlined in this book.

SAS University Edition

If you are using SAS University Edition to access data and run your programs, then please check the SAS University Edition page to ensure that the software contains the product or products that you need to run the code: www.sas.com/universityedition.

Code examples are designed to run against the sample data provided.

SAS Visual Analytics Trial

To access a free trial of SAS Visual Analytics software you can go to: www.sas.com/va

Samples in this book are designed to work with SAS Visual Analytics version 8.2.

We Want to Hear from You

SAS Press books are written *by* SAS Users *for* SAS Users. We welcome your participation in their development and your feedback on SAS Press books that you are using. Please visit sas.com/books
 to do the following:

- Sign up to review a book
- Recommend a topic
- Request information on how to become a SAS Press author
- Provide feedback on a book

Do you have questions about a SAS Press book that you are reading? Contact the author through saspress@sas.com or https://support.sas.com/author_feedback.

SAS has many resources to help you find answers and expand your knowledge. If you need additional help, see our list of resources: sas.com/books.

If you have questions about accessibility features in this document, please contact saspress@sas.com.

About the Author

 Travis Murphy has worked for more than 15 years in data warehousing, business intelligence, and analytics. At SAS Institute, Travis has held presales, technical account management, business solution management, and marketing roles focused on data visualization tools. Travis is always working to better communicate the value and insight of data using software tools and to get business users and stakeholders more involved in the use of data. Travis has presented at SAS Global Forums, user conferences, and SAS marketing roadshows, where he continues to evangelize the benefits of approachable analytics and data visualization. Your comments and questions are valued and encouraged. For more information and to contact the author please visit: http://support.sas.com/murphy.

Acknowledgments

Each book is born from an idea, and this book was no different: the idea that all users of SAS should have a book to show how all users of SAS can build infographics. SAS is a collection of powerful applications that a business user can pick up and get value from right away. In fact, a business user should be able to pick up SAS and use a variety of the tools to improve their skills from beginner, through intermediate, through to advanced. This book takes in more ideas than what I alone could provide, so I would like to acknowledge some other people who had impact on this book.

This book would not be possible without the support of my family. My wife, Emily, and sons, William and Edward, traveled the globe to support my dreams, and have kept telling me to keep writing even when it got a bit tiresome. To Dad, Mum, and my siblings, thanks for teaching me that being creative is a must, and adventure is everywhere. This adventure continues…

Specific thanks go to the following people:

William Murphy – My son and graphic designer. Thanks for his assistance from the cover design to the last-minute image creation for the galleries in the book. Nothing was too much trouble to him. Thank-you.

Robert Allison – Mr. SAS Graph, provided the samples and built the code that I required for the dashboards that I used in the relevant examples. His endless source of examples online have inspired me over many years, and when I needed some help, he could not have been more generous with his time, advice, and assistance.

Falko Schulz – Falko is such a talented software developer who works on the SAS team developing SAS Visual Analytics. On top of this, he can translate a story into the software, and his samples used in this book provided many ideas and questions. Many years ago, he taught me that SAS can do anything. So, since then, I dream big!

Also, the following people I would like to thank: the SAS Publishing team who was tremendously supportive during the publishing process, the R&D team at SAS for their constant support, the broader product management and product marketing teams at SAS for their assistance and support, the SAS Communities team for encouraging me to post, and, finally, the SAS team that I have worked with each day during my career. I thank SAS Australia and New Zealand for the great roles that I have had in my time there and with SAS Canada for the opportunity to work abroad. Some of the great work that we have done together has made its way into this book.

Part 1

Concepts

In **Part 1** we introduce the basic concepts about infographics and why they are important. We explore origins, types and considerations when designing infographics. We discuss where SAS can add value to the process of creating infographics. You will see how to drive additional value from big data and better engage your stakeholders.

Chapter 1

Getting Started

Introduction

"A picture is worth a thousand words". This overused phrase is almost mundane these days. However, it is truer than ever in history. A picture is worth a billion words might be a better representation of what is today's reality. There are many reasons why this is the case, and we will explore this further in the chapters ahead.

The world is at a point where the attention span of a consumer is only about eight seconds (McSpadden, 2015). If something doesn't grab their attention, chances are they will move on. Not only will they move on, but most of the time they won't come back. This has created a shift in the massive growth of infographics to quickly show data-driven visuals for immediate impact. According to Just and Ludtke (2010), there is a reason for this growth in infographics:

> "Now you can circumvent written language to a large extent. A lot of printed words are there to describe things that occur spatially. In many cases a picture is worth a thousand words. Now we can generate these pictures and graphics and we can convey them to other people very easily. I think it's inevitable that visual media are going to become more important in conveying ideas and not just about raging fires."
> Marcel Just, Center for Cognitive Brain Imaging at Carnegie Mellon University, 2010.

As the quote implies, and as many instinctive and logical proof points show, visualization is a more effective way of getting a reaction from the audience. It is proven that data presented visually is more easily processed by the brain than looking at the tabular format or words alone (Dale, 1969).

Business analysts need to adapt to this shift in the audience's attention span and combine visuals with the massive amount of available data. We need to combine creative infographics with big data to take advantage of the opportunities that the data presents. The boardroom, just like the classroom, has a much shorter attention span for consuming information and reaching the "Aha" moment as fast as possible. The emergence and growth of many data visualization tools have placed infographics and data visualization at the forefront when considering business intelligence solutions.

Infographics Today

All infographics have their place, and when used correctly, they can have a great impact on the intended audience. The infographics outlined in this book combine artistic elements (such as clip art and background images) with data-driven content from the corporate data warehouse or the big data platform. Traditionally, the infographic creator/author needed to spend a large amount of time with tools such as Microsoft Excel or certain programming languages to develop and craft the correct data to support the right visualization. This is not the case anymore.

What has changed is the vast increase in data: the volume, the variety, and the velocity. The Internet of Things and surrounding applications guarantee the continued growth in data assets. The importance of data visualization will be the difference between noticing a pattern or missing a pattern altogether. To add to this, business analysts need to do what they did in multiple pages in a dashboard now in eight seconds to capture the audience. Business analysts must provide insight and create a reason for the audience to click through to more detailed information. This is where the infographic comes in.

 One only caveat is that pictures and visualizations themselves should not impede the message or the clarity of the information being communicated. I know from personal experience, working on many data warehouse projects, that all stakeholders, whether executive or line manager, need to be guided on a path, a repeatable path, to the insight that is being communicated from the data platform. SAS has been a leader in data visualization for more than 40 years. Over the years, SAS tools have improved so as to be more approachable for more people within an organization.

Today, analysts do not have to write code to get great visualization from the data. They don't have to spend hours using scripts and spreadsheets to craft the data into a usable format. The analyst can start to be more creative on the visual layer and to place better visualization in their infographics. This book is not focused on the theory of design for infographics. I will leave that to the graphic designers, data journalists, and visual artists of the world. This book focuses on the SAS analytic engine and associated software to make extremely powerful tools available to the business analyst to better create infographics.

The Goal

Of course, there are other tools that are very well-suited for a graphic artist, and they too have a barrier to entry with many years of education required to become proficient. On the flipside, our aim is to create a business-ready environment to take some of the benefits of the infographics to the enterprise stakeholders or the c-level executive in the boardroom. Today more than ever before, organizations must continue to innovate in methods and approaches on how we capture the attention of our business stakeholders. This book shows you that you have an option, right now, with your current SAS investment.

The best way to set the scene for what is being proposed in this book is to look at the final output first. Figure 1.1 is a typical example of an output type that is created in this book:

Figure 1.1 Sample Infographic Created with SAS and Microsoft Office

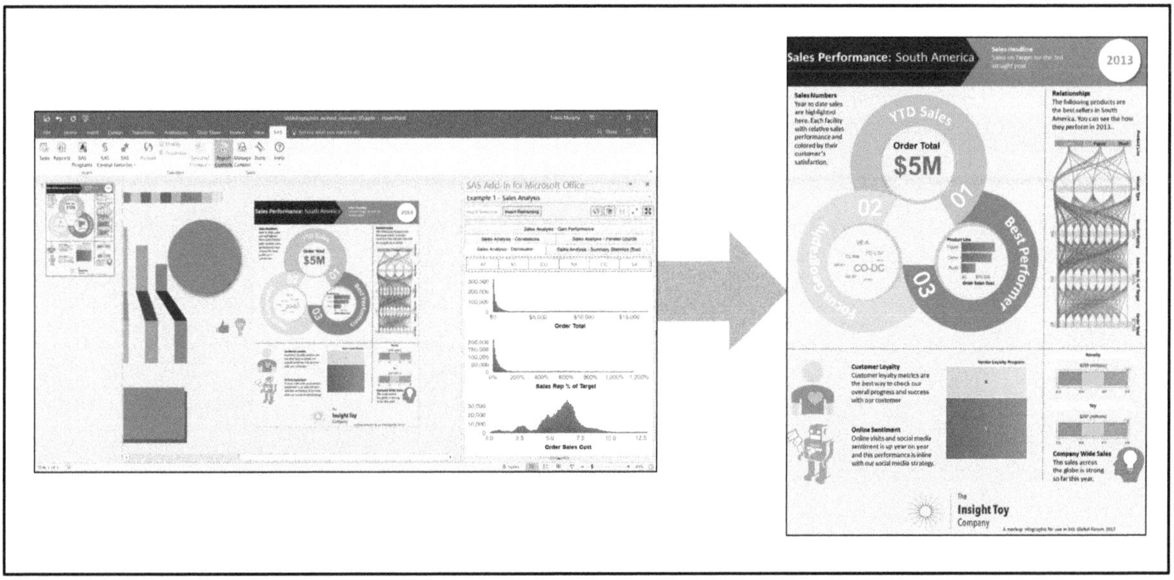

As seen in Figure 1.1, this book will allow you to create infographics for business teams to share corporate data with the consumers of that data, and will achieve this by using the power of SAS and the familiarity of Microsoft Office. This book will show some examples and different approaches to achieve this goal. Before we jump into the solution, let's look at the infographic in more detail.

Chapter 2

Visual Tour of Infographics

Overview

The purpose of this chapter is to provide a gallery of examples of information graphics in the world today, and to introduce the concept of business information graphic versus artistic information graphic. This chapter will use visual examples to assist the reader in understanding the potential and power of infographics. These examples will not be specific to SAS. However, they could be based on SAS or on third-party creation tools. This chapter will be used to set up the reader's expectations of what they can achieve using such tools.

Audience

If the user is an experienced SAS user, this chapter will provide a frame of reference for what they can achieve later in this book. Similarly, if the reader is a novice SAS user or an intermediate SAS user, then this chapter provides a visual reference of what can be achieved by reading this book.

Power of Infographics

Infographics combine art and science to produce something that is not unlike a dashboard. The main difference from a dashboard is the subjective data and the narrative or story, which enhances the data-driven visual and engages the audience quickly through highlighting the required context.

Infographics can be used with your day-to-day business analytics information that you create and distribute at work. Consider infographics as another way to engage your stakeholders.

Interest in infographics is on the rise over recent years, and people strive to tell better and more engaging stories to their audience. Using a simple Google Trends search, you can see in Figure 2.1 the increase in the number of searches for the term "Infographic" over the number of searches for the term "Data Visualization."

Figure 2.1. Search Data for the Terms "Data Visualization" and "Infographic"

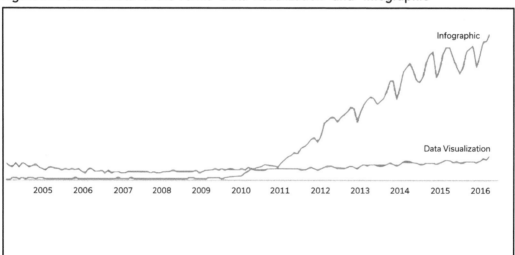

Figure 2.1 demonstrates an increased interest in infographics. Let's review the important attributes of a successful infographic.

Common elements of most infographics:

- **visually appealing** – always the goal, but not always achieved.
- **easy to understand** – this gets lost sometimes, but simplicity is often the best rule.
- **fast insight** – this is really the core goal of an infographic.

At the center of all infographics is the topic: a central question to be answered or a topic to be discussed. Selecting a central question or question to answer is crucial to the success of an infographic. Those that fail to answer a question, or present little information on a niche topic, often show more style than substance and fail to capture the reader's attention.

Origins of Infographics

The infographic is not a new concept, and visual communication has been a cornerstone of humanity. From cave paintings around 30,000 BC to the seafarers, astronomers and explorers of the modern world, maps and drawings have been used to take complex information and distill it into consumable information. Ancient civilizations have used drawings to communicate important events and to capture history for future generations or even to communicate to the hereafter.

More clearly aligned with the modern use and design of infographics, Figure 2.2 shows "Diagram of the Causes of Mortality in the Army in the East." It was created by Florence Nightingale from data collected during the Crimean War (1854–56). It was reportedly presented to the UK Parliament and was used to highlight health data. The result was a clear story for the politicians and stakeholders, which was more impactful due to the visualization.

Figure 2.2. Early Infographic Example: "Diagram of the Causes of Mortality in the Army in the East" (Image credit: Florence Nightingale, 1858)

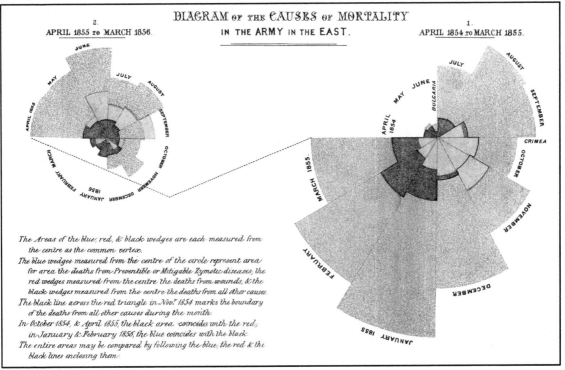

Types of Infographics

There are different types of infographics that can be summarized in broad categories: artistic and business. The artistic infographic is one in which graphic designers take information from authors and create a very artistic visual. This visual could be hung on the wall as a poster or put on an internet home page to support a headline. The other is the business infographic. This is a very structured visual and an extension of the dashboard concept. A dashboard can be an infographic, as well. However, in general, dashboards are more about data (including slice and dice data) than about being subjective. The dashboard is often the one-stop shop for self-service business intelligence. There is also a place for the artistic infographics that we have come to love. Let's take a quick tour of these ever-increasing visual elements and why they are used.

Artistic Infographics

Many people think of infographics in the form of popular posters that are seen on kitchen or living room walls. I love how the data of today has been used for data driven artistic expression, however, this is a centuries-old approach. The modern take on this artistic expression has achieved popularity via the crowdfunding world. These projects have been created to tell complex themes and to bring to life what the crowdfunding backers want. These infographics generally have the following characteristics:

- aesthetically pleasing
- highly creative bespoke designs
- layered storytelling

Many of the examples I found to reference here were just too long vertically to insert into the book and this aspect ratio the infographic posters makes these perfect for displaying a on your wall at home or office. Therefore, I have obtained help to create some examples for use here.

The following are a few examples to set your frame of reference for artistic infographics (Figures 2.3–2.5).

Figure 2.3. Horror Movie Genre Poster Example (Image credit: W. Murphy, 2018)

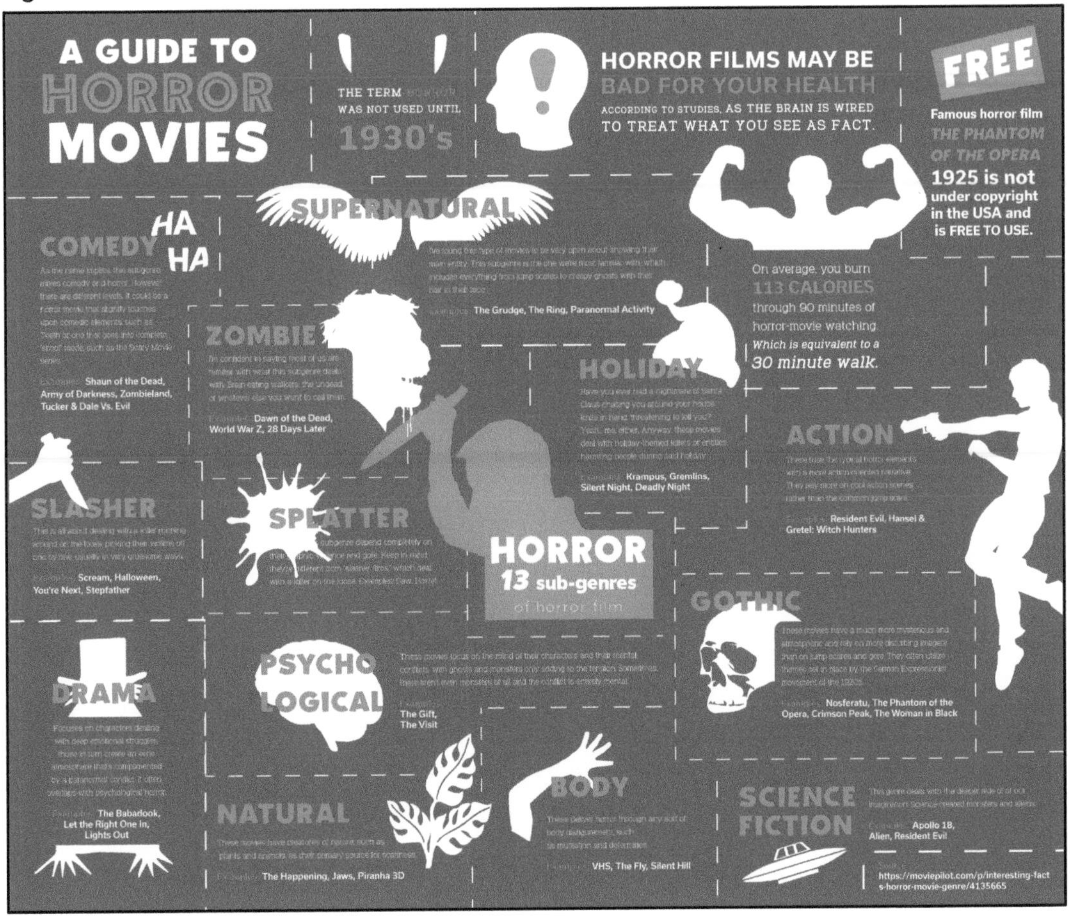

This entertainment topic gets a lot of attention in the infographics world. This horror film poster is ready for any movie buff's game room wall.

Figure 2.4. Space Rocks Infographic (Image credit: W. Murphy, 2018)

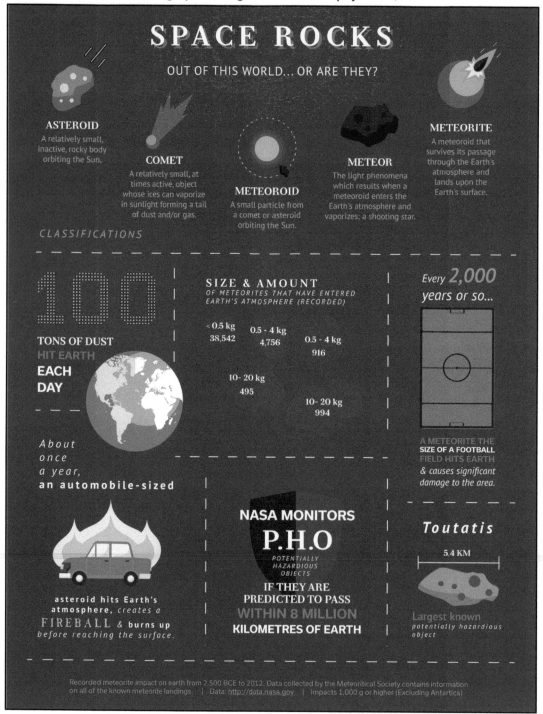

Here is another example of an entertaining infographic that is suitable for framing.

Figure 2.5. Volcano Infographic (Image credit: W. Murphy, 2018)

The preceding figure shows an example of volcanic activity across the globe. The data was analyzed with SAS and the result was merged and further illustrated with desktop publishing software.

Business Infographics

Business infographics have been used for a long time in the form of rich presentations. Aggregating information and making it more digestible is not new for business. Over the years, we have used overheads, chalkboards, white boards, and even butcher's paper for business presentations. In the digital world, presentation has become an obsession, and many people devote their careers to crafting stories from complex business data.

Figure 2.6 uses the engine metaphor to show the complex process of turning data into actionable insights. The engine metaphor is a great way to connect new concepts to a viewer's existing understanding.

Figure 2.6. Data Decisioning Pump (Image credit: M. Turner, 2017)

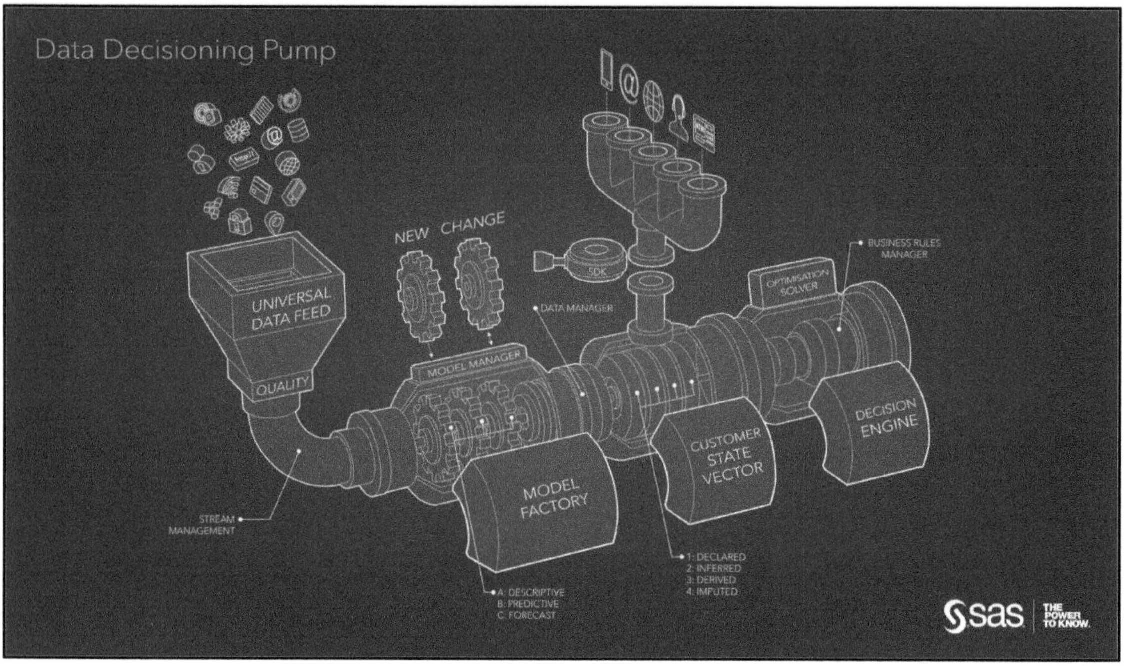

This presentation example from SAS UK uses an engine metaphor to show how analytics and data can drive marketing interactions with customers (Turner, 2017).

Figure 2.7 is still a structured layout, which is consistent with business infographics. However, it is more of a repetition of core facts about a topic, and in this case, it focuses on a core theme: top 100 baby names. This infographic uses dashboard style objects (word clouds and ranked tables) to highlight the performance of names over time. Trends, which is a traditional business data visualization technique, show the performance of certain names over time.

Figure 2.7. Popular Baby Names in a Word Cloud (Image credit: W. Murphy, 2018)

Figure 2.8 is a very traditional example of a business infographic which combines data, images, and text to highlight the topic in a structured way. It is simple, attractive, and focused on a single topic, which in this example is a customer happiness survey.

Figure 2.8. Business Infographic Example

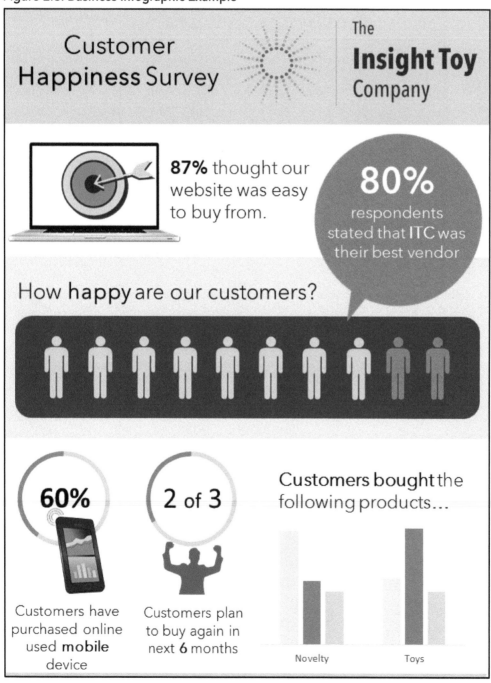

Information Fragments: A Common Subcategory

Cutting across all infographics is the concept of an information fragment (infofragment) or snippet. This type of infographic is used as an engaging or entertaining entry point into a complex topic (such as news feeds about world issues and social justice), or a novelty item (such as B2C or B2B offers). Often, the infofragment contains just enough information to attract attention, but rarely enough information to provide the complete story or context. Infofragments are often used as "clickbait" on the newer devices like smart phones or tablets.

Figure 2.9 shows a set of infofragments that support a single statistic about STEM education.

Figure 2.9. A sample infofragment (Image credit: W. Murphy, 2018)

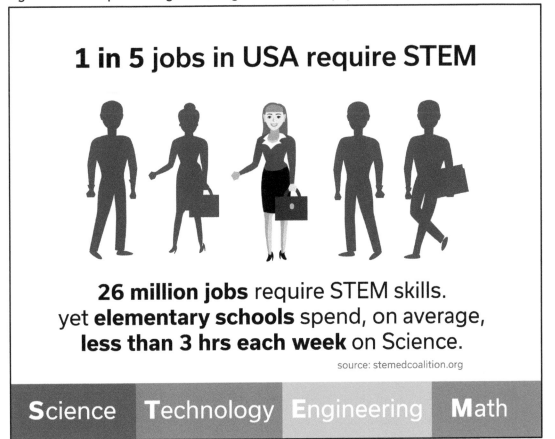

Infofragments are the start of the information journey. Where to next? This is the teaser to which the user responds with a click or swipe to get more information.

Figure 2.10 is another example of an infofragment:

Figure 2.10. Infofragment about the Environment (Image credit: W. Murphy, 2018)

Infofragments successfully capture issues in core points that can be easily displayed, communicated, consumed, and shared. This infofragment provides the desired entry point and encourages the social sharing of this core insight to broader networks that promote the cause.

Figure 2.11 shows a style that is consistent with typical displays of election results around the globe and in real time on news channels. The infofragment anchors the story and broadens the story's reach with matching social media tiles that are shared on corporate websites.

Figure 2.11. SAS Example of Election Results (Image credit: R. Allison, 2016)

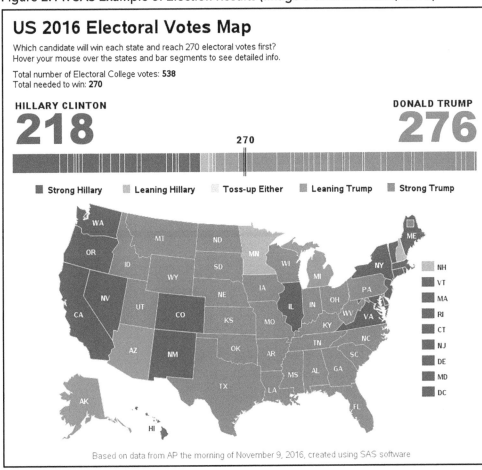

The BBC uses rich visualizations online and in the news broadcast to better engage with the audience but to differentiate itself from other news services. (Farnsworth, 2017)

SAS Sees the Value in Infographics

SAS is also using more infographics to communicate to our customers in a less formal and more approachable way. In my experience in marketing with SAS, and in posting on social media regularly (with LinkedIn and Twitter for business networks), these infographics have been more popular and have produced higher engagement than words alone or even traditional banner images. This testimonial is based on my own online profiles used since 2015.

Some examples of these types of corporate infographics from SAS follow.

Figure 2.12. SAS Infographic for 40th Birthday Celebrations in 2016 (Image credit: SAS, 2016)

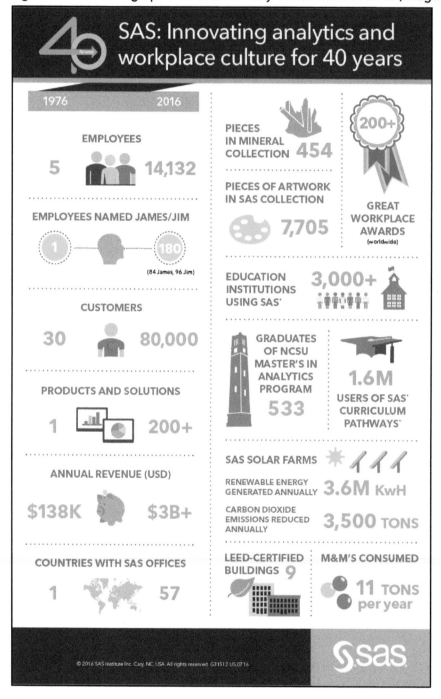

This infographic fits a huge amount of disparate fun facts about SAS on a single easy-to-read and share display. One fact that stands out to me is the amount of M&Ms that we consumed per year: 11 tons. Yum!

Figure 2.13 shows an infographic that was created to advertise the SAS Global Forum 2018 and the experience of previous attendees.

Figure 2.13. SAS Infographic (Image credit: SAS, 2018)

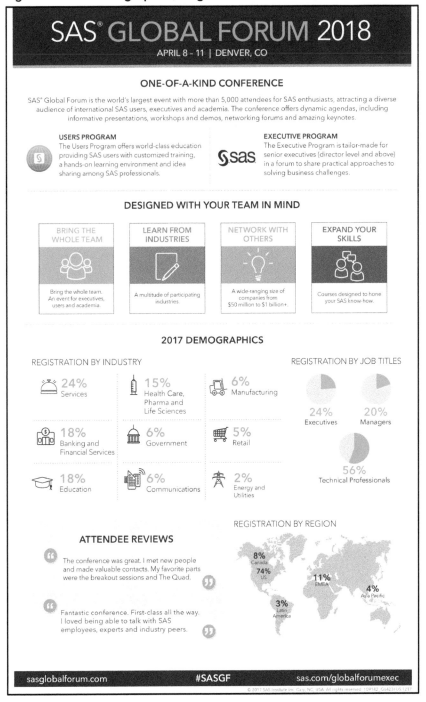

The following infographic shown in Figure 2.14 helps communicate the value and message to the market about SAS and our modern analytics engine SAS Viya.

Figure 2.14. SAS Infographic about SAS Viya (Image credit: SAS, 2017)

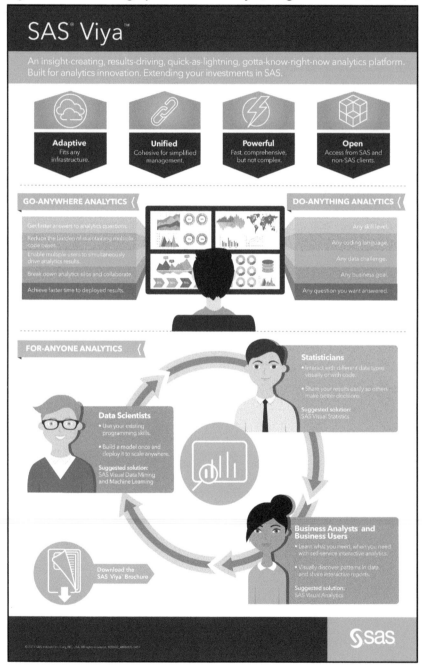

For years, SAS has created a plethora of product documentation, white papers and detailed capability studies. Now, SAS looks to add more approachable entry points to these traditional assets by leveraging the infographic. SAS is making the content more approachable and if more information is required by the reader, they can click through to more traditional documentation sources.

SAS software, in combination with tools like Microsoft Office, can also be used to achieve a wide range of outputs like the preceding examples of infographics. I encourage you to test the boundaries in finding a way use SAS tools to represent data that have highly visual requirements.

Art versus Science

Overview

The aim of this chapter is to outline the importance of design and the ability to strike a balance between a robust and repeatable data-driven approach when designing an infographic. This chapter explores the combination of being a data artist while still being a data scientist. We look at how graphic design sensibilities are useful in business today when they don't take away from the clarity of the message being shared from the data.

Audience

This chapter is designed for all SAS skill levels and is an important foundation for the remainder of the book.

Artistic Freedom versus Communication

Data analysts struggle with today's requirements to present data in a highly visual and appealing manner. I remember predictions that the shift from print to online media would shatter the graphic design industry. What I saw instead was a huge opportunity for online content to apply visual elements in order to compete and remain engaging. I believe this has been proven with the rise of graphic art in today's world especially in marketing practices.

We might have heard about and read the theory that people understand visual communication better than any other format. In my research for this book, I came across many perspectives that share this basic point of view. Science tells us that half the human brain is involved with visual processing (Merieb and Hoehn, 2007) and that 70% of all sensory receptors are located in the eyes (Merieb and Hoehn, 2007), which tells us that humans are all about the visuals. If humans can process context and get a sense of a visual scene in one-tenth of a second, this knowledge should motivate information producers to make their information more easily understood (Semetko and Scammell, 2012). According to Dale (1969), humans retain 30% what they see, 20% what they hear, and 10% what they read (see Figure 3.1 for a conceptual illustration of this concept).

Figure 3.1 Human Retention of Information (Image credit: W. Murphy, 2018)

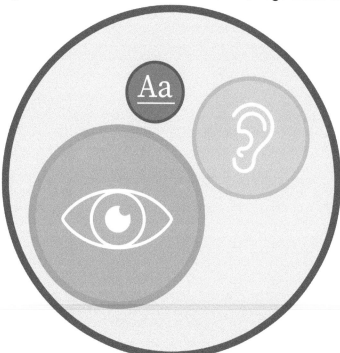

I have seen similar numbers that report as high as 80% on the visual component. (ETHOS3, 2016) Even if this statistic is close to accurate, then communicating data should be done through engaging and clear visuals . Otherwise, you risk becoming white noise in a world where attention spans are shorter than ever. The key to being relevant and understood is creating an information graphic with a balance of pleasing aesthetics and clarity of message.

Traditional Personas

Traditional personas are worth exploring in the context of infographics. They are the Artist, the Scientist, the Data Artist, and Audience. All aim to provide insight with varied levels of restraint.

Artist

The artist might feel free to create without restriction. The artist might create for personal satisfaction first, and the audience second. The artist typically creates customized designs and unique works.

Scientist

The scientist derives proof from the data. In this context, the scientist is a data analyst who is comfortable with the data at the raw level and who has the mathematical skills to understand underlying patterns. They have invested in skills to work from the data up to ensure the integrity in all they do. Their sound knowledge of the data enables them to answer critical questions from their peers in business.

Data Artist: The Combination/Hybrid

The combination of the Artist with the Scientist produces the Data Artist. Although this role demands both skills sets, one person might not have both skills equally. In this case, the person in the role might perform at an optimum level in the area of expertise, but seek help from others when necessary in the other. For example, if they are less scientific, then they need help with being supported here. If they are less artistic, then support is needed in this area.

I believe we all have some level of data artist inside us, and, when supported correctly, we can develop and encourage these skills to come out and enhance our interactions with our stakeholders.

Audience

This is the key persona when designing visual communications. We all play this role at different times, even if our primary role is Artist, Scientist, or Data Artist. We all consume information that others create. This persona should always be in the forefront of our minds when working on any data-driven communications.

Traditional Outputs

There are many information outputs that are designed for the consumer, and great effort is required to create these outputs for a particular set of data. There is also often an overlap of effort to create the outputs. As information developers, people prefer their favorite form of output, or have only a particular output option in their skill set or their software stack.

Spreadsheets

The spreadsheet is great for personal productivity. However, it might not be great for the enterprise. Spreadsheets have been a staple in data processing for decades. Personal freedom is high due to the flexibility of changing the data and slices of the data that match the information developer's understanding of the business requirements and rules. However, spreadsheets are not easy to scale to today's data loads.

Dashboards

Dashboards are great for guided analysis. However, they are not always easy to understand. They are often too hard to navigate for the business user (the audience), and they are too limited for the scientist.

Reports

A report often takes the form of a desktop-published report such as a monthly sales report or a visually appealing dashboard that provides self-service. This has been widely used in the business intelligence world to drive repetition and scale.

Email

Email is another staple for communicating between members of the business teams. However, one might find the data-driven insights to be somewhat untrustworthy. Where did the numbers come from? Email is not an easy medium to communicate insight to the audience because the "Aha" is often buried in text.

Presentations

Business teams have used presentations for communication purposes for decades. Presentations, of course, vary by the author. Often, the data that is presented becomes quickly outdated, and the author must manually update everything for the next meeting. The presentation slides force the audience to sit through information that does not interest them, which often means they stop paying attention before the insight is shared, which is not good for presenter or audience.

Infographics

Infographics are an output which has gained popularity in the business world in recent years. They have proven to be a great way to engage when used along with other traditional outputs. Infographic principles can be used to enrich the more traditional outputs.

Flexible Tools

Information requirements are shifting, and, more and more, the toolset needs to adapt to ensure the availability of traditional and less traditional methods. The tools must be flexible in order to account for all the above personas' needs. The tools should augment their skills in areas in which they need support. Also, the tools must provide the depth and breadth that are necessary to support users' knowledge and expertise.

To achieve the balance between art and science, you can leverage the enterprise strength of the SAS Visual Analytics engine with the popular personal productivity tools of Microsoft Office. Check the tools sections of the book for more information, including the version numbers of the software that is used in this book.

Changing Technology Landscape

Overview

This chapter talks about the shifting sands of technology and the impact on infographic design and consumption. Information delivery has evolved from its origins in spreadsheets, PDF documents and Adobe Flash deliverables and has moved to the world that we are in today with interactive technologies like HTML5. The movement from static deliverables toward a visual and interactive medium challenges all companies in the technology industry to adapt to new demands or risk becoming obsolete.

The aim of this chapter is to provide the reader with a reference of why this is important today more than ever and how the Internet of Things (IoT) and digital culture has demanded a new approach in order to engage stakeholders. Big data in the era of IoT requires that a story is told using visuals to elevate the narrative to an audience who lacks the time and skill in analyzing the results. Spreadsheets no longer "cut the mustard." Data visualization and infographics are a great way to derive value from this vast data.

Audience

This chapter will be interesting to novice SAS users who are starting to understand the importance of technology for enabling the business to achieve their goals. Furthermore, advanced SAS programmers will see the business context and the impact of technology.

Technology

In recent years, many new tools (open source and from vendors) have created a wave of interest like never before. Some might say that the plethora of new tools is due to innovation and disruption. However, I say that the large number of tools has responded to the growth of data. The explosion of data to be precise. More data requires new ways to think about how to make sense of it all. According to Jim Goodnight, SAS CEO (Shaw, 2017):

"Over the past 40 years we have seen visualization go from standard X, Y charts to dashboards and scorecards but frankly these do not work for dimensional data – it's big data in overdrive."

SAS has been quick to adapt to this shift in big data with continuous improvement around how to apply analytics to this growth in data. The examples in the book show the combination of big data analytics and traditional techniques to support the belief that having the right options for all analysts is the correct approach. Many tools in the market today look to solve some, rarely all, of what is needed for all analytics users in an enterprise. The right tools should be selected according to the skills of the user who is analyzing the data.

I am totally onboard with this approach. Also, customers tell me that big data is not a problem for them, and they have all they need to make their decisions. I would question these beliefs. More data is available today than what organizations are using, and traditional tools for data analysis really can't keep up. I believe that one reason infographics are on the rise is because of this struggle to leverage the vast amount of available data.

Market Trends for Data Visualization

Along with big data, other technology elements keep moving and will continue to drive innovation in the requirements for information developers and the audience. Here are the technology elements that can help deliver information:

- Mobile – create and consume content anywhere at anytime.
- Self-service – provides analytics, data wrangling and blending to all users.
- Cloud – removes barriers to entry for business teams.
- Cognitive – helps, wherever possible, to use machine learning and to strive toward artificial intelligence.

In her presentation at the 2017 SAS Global Forum in Orlando, Florida, Amanda Farnsworth said that when she started her current role at the BBC in 2013, she observed users "switch from accessing from desktop to accessing on mobile, and we were thinking of screens that shape, and tabs, and clicking, and interactivity, and the audience had to work pretty hard to find some really important information" (Farnsworth, 2017).

In the same presentation, Farnsworth continued with noting where we are today:

"Now we think in the screen like this (mobile/smart phone), and scrolling, we have to adapt and unlearn some of things we used to know about the job we do, and learn new techniques to engage an audience on smartphone" (Farnsworth, 2017).

These quotations are validation that we need to change the way we think about communicating with stakeholders in our businesses and to our customers or citizens. News is such a competitive industry, and we can all look to apply these lessons from data journalists to other industries. No wonder this was such a popular talk at 2017 SAS Global Forum: many industries are taking notice on how to engage customers with data and graphics.

API Economy and the Age of Analytics

The rise of the API (Application Programming Interface) has seen an urgency for integration. It is no longer acceptable to be a silo in an organization. A data visualization toolset, and more broadly, an analytics engine, needs to ensure that they can consume and be consumed by other technologies today. The API economy is seeing very focused development of capabilities by both start-ups and Fortune 500s. I have former SAS colleague who is involved with one such start-up and they continue to grow.

With these advances, we also see the age of analytics (Mckinsey, 2016), which exceeds the scope of this book. Analytics continues to be a disruptor in many traditional markets such as driverless cars or Uber to the taxi industry. As an illustration of disruption in the field of data visualization, bots are being used by organizations to suggest possible infographic designs and insights for social media-ready data visualizations. Bots are even used to automate publishing from existing information feeds. Analytics underpins the ability for true automation and is the key to machine-to-machine communication. Analytics also supports the drive toward artificial intelligence (AI).

Technology Improvements Continue to Drive Innovation

At the heart of these shifts is advancement in technology: the cost of computing and the speed of computing. Moore's law (projection of compute power doubling every two years) is a well-known theory on computing power (Britannica, 2017). Whether you agree with the specifics of the theory, it illustrates the point well: compute power continues to increase. The cost of this compute power is also reducing over time. This cost reduction opens up more available computing power for more users and more organizations. Combined with the growth in available data, and the lower cost, less technically complex deployment of this compute power via cloud platforms and SaaS/PaaS vendors, we see more organizations looking to apply analytics to problems that they were not looking at in the past.

The challenge and opportunity for IT vendors is to remove all barriers to access, deployment, and management of the analytics platform for organizations. Innovation is key to taking advantage of these technological advances. SAS continues to invest in Research and Development and to innovate on all layers of the analytics platform to assist customers to take advantage of this shift in technologies.

The release of SAS Viya as part of the SAS platform, which is used in this book's infographics examples, was created to embrace these technology improvements outlined here.

Chapter 5

General Considerations for Designing Infographics

Overview

This chapter highlights some of the considerations needed to get the most from infographics in your business. The information in this chapter is based on my research for this book and on my experience working with customers over the years to communicate insight from their data.

Audience

This is aimed at all SAS users who might be new to infographics.

Analytics for Everyone

Similar to how data analysts benefit from a visual interpretation of data, a business user or executive stakeholder might also benefit from data visualization.

The data alone is difficult to engage with for most consumers of data. It is not impossible, as proven by the spreadsheet culture that has become entrenched in organizations over the past 30 years. The time spent in learning the spreadsheet's context for the data often exceeds the time spent in making business decisions from the data.

In the past, the spreadsheet was a useful and acceptable option because the volume of data was small enough so that the user could get oriented and learn the context fairly quickly. Today, this is not the case. The volume of data is too large and varied to use this approach.

Data analysis might be complex, but it does not have to be "ugly." This complexity can be reduced by using repeatable and approachable visualizations. Approachable software, such as SAS, can introduce users to concepts that are learned and unlocked by seeing and understanding analytic models through visualization. In short, the business data might change for each business question. However, the business analyst learns how to interpret the visualization in context of the business data. Data visualization can drastically reduce the learning curve for the entire organization. This is true self-service analytics.

Data Visualization 101: The Basics

It is important to set a few rules about data visualization before we get too far downstream with infographic design.

Data Accuracy

According to *Cool Infographics: Effective Communication with Data Visualization and Design* (Krum, 2014), the most important aspect of any infographic is accuracy. Everything else is secondary. The best way to ensure that accuracy is achieved is to understand the data the best you can. Therefore, you need to explore the data first. You need to check the numbers from many angles and confirm your understanding and assumptions. Then, you decide on the important numbers that you want to highlight. Finally, you decide how to communicate the important numbers in your infographic.

Storytelling

Telling the right story is supported by specific options that you have for displaying the data, but choosing the right graph to visualize your data can be hard. It is easier when you consider the goal of your visualization. This handy visual, designed by Dr. Andrew Abela and shown in Figure 5.1, provides some ideas on deciding what visualization will tell the story that you want to tell. Of course, there are many more options that are available to visualize your data. However, this approach can be useful for starting to frame the data visualization options.

Figure 5.1. Chart Suggestions (Image © Dr. Andrew V. Abela, 2017, www.ExtremePresentation.com)

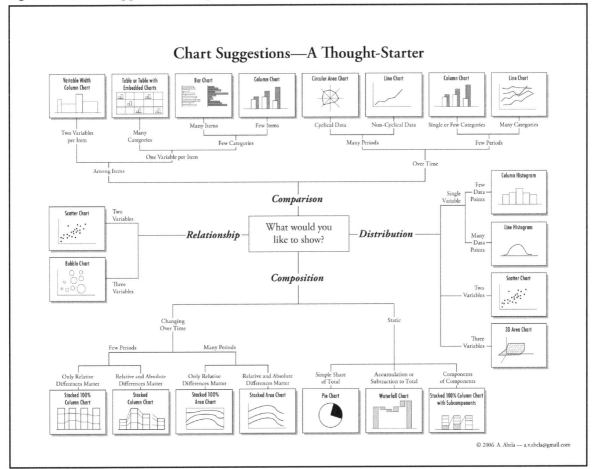

Foundations of Visual Perception

In his book, *Information Dashboard Design*, Stephen Few discusses the Gestalt Principles of Visual Perception. Research from the Gestalt school of psychology in 1912 focused on how we perceive pattern, form, and organization, and many of their findings remain in practice today (Few, 2006).

From my research, how you decide on displaying the information in your infographic should be based on your knowledge of how the audience processes the information you are highlighting. Some ideas to consider are the proximity of related data, the use of similar shapes and colors for related data, and the grouping and connection of data together for clear relationships.

As highlighted by Few:

> "Two of the greatest challenges... are to make the most important data stand out from the rest, and to arrange what is often a great deal of disparate information in a way that makes sense" (Few, 2006).

Elements of an Infographic

The following types of elements are a good foundation for data visualization and infographics design: quantitative elements and subjective elements.

Quantitative: Data-Driven Elements

Choose the right visual or graphic to fit the situation. Choose carefully what you are aiming to highlight. Also, if a graph is not the best way to communicate the data insight, use an image or a high-level number to highlight the context of the data, according to the data. Dynamic text can also be powerful according to the data selected. Use a data comprehension test before you build the data visualization. This means will your audience understand what you are showing in your design.

Subjective: Creative Elements

Icons can assist with getting the point across quickly and can act as a reference, analogy, or metaphor. Symbolism and metaphors can be a great way to anchor the message of your infographic, and often this means custom icons or images. Text is also a great way to add some context to the infographic and to provide a layer of understanding. This includes title text and explanatory comments.

Branding creates an identity for your content. This could also be a way of aligning your themes to the corporate branding of your organization by using the logo or corporate colors. Colors do matter. Use color to highlight data, rather than to distract the audience. We all struggle with this fine line of color and often use too much color. More is not always better.

User experience is sometimes misplaced or forgotten, but ultimately user experience is what makes the infographic hit its mark. What story are you telling, and how easy is it for the user to see, without you being there to guide them. The best infographics are the ones that work on different levels. Someone who has a quick glance gets something from it, and someone who spends more time gets something extra.

Designing an Infographic

Here is the process that I use to design an infographic:

1. **Idea** – Research and decide on what questions might be interesting to answer. Also, what data do you need in order to answer the questions?
2. **Design** – Use a whiteboard or a piece of paper to get the ideas out of your head and into the real world. This step should provide ideas for topic, context, and questions that I want to answer or highlight, and design ideas for the infographic.
3. **Discover** – Do some iterations and use trial-and-error to see whether your ideas are achievable. Do some data analysis and understand what is possible in achieving your design.
4. **Deliver** – How will you deliver the infographic, is it on-demand, or shared as a static image? What will the infographic look like, is it an infofragment, or a poster? Patience and persistence will ensure that you build the best infographic.
5. **Share** – Publish the infographic, and get it out to your audience. You can use a small group first if you have the time, and this helps you catch anything that you might have missed before publishing to all.
6. **Refine** – Gather inputs from everywhere, refine your design, and build again. The feedback loop is important. With each iteration, you get more of an idea of what your audience wants and how you can

deliver the infographic better each time.

Figure 5.2 shows a graphical summary of the process:

Figure 5.2. Infographic Creation Process

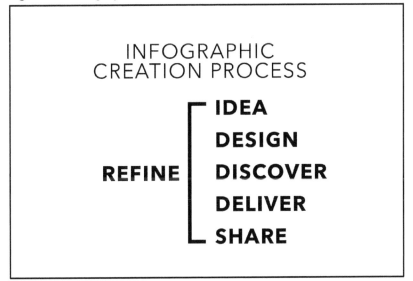

And yes, this creation process could be used for dashboards or other information products. However, it is very useful when designing infographics of all types.

Experimenting is key in hitting the mark with your audience. In marketing to your customers, there are many approaches to ensure that your message hits the mark, like using A-B testing methods to select the best marketing message for a particular audience. This can provide the best "bang for buck" and make your message hit the mark with your customer. Similarly, when designing information graphics, we need to test and refine the message and the story with our intended audience.

Designing for Audience

For years, I have used a simple, layered approach to designing information products. Here is a simple workflow for your audience to follow their "line of thought":

1. **Infofragment** – This is the snippet of key information that hooks viewers and gets them asking for more.
2. **Infographic** – The infographic will provide more layers and information than the infofragment, as the viewer investigates further.
3. **Dashboard** – The dashboard provides the viewer with self-service analysis and interactive slice-and-dice.
4. **Data** – Often, the viewer will require proof that the data in the dashboard is accurate, and they get this by seeing the detailed data, in context.
5. **Sharing** – Collaboration and sharing is key to all steps, and collaboration should be consistent from start to finish, as this sharing builds trust between audience and the data visualization.

Figure 5.3 shows a graphical summary of the process:

Figure 5.3. Information Navigation Flow

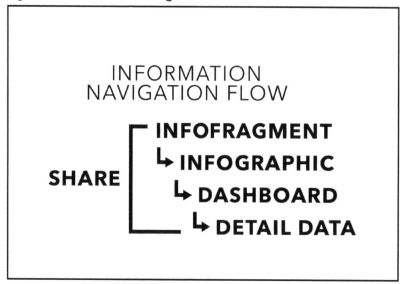

Designing for the Non-designer

You don't have to be a graphic designer to make effective infographics. However, some self-education is a great step forward. Get inspiration and be creative like a child. This is true with data visualization, and one way to do this is to increase your inputs. Consider feedback from colleagues, websites and magazines, wherever ideas come. Then, capture them on paper, the whiteboard, or digital tablet.

Here are some design tips for the non-designer:

- Ensure that your story is clear. No matter how much extra effort goes into the polish or sizzle, the story is always key.
- Train yourself in some design principles if you can. It helps!
- Professional design teams can help add pizzazz. They take your idea and add the polish to make it shine.
- "Aspire to inspire" is design-speak for designing to make a difference to your audience . Try to make your infographic matter.
- Less can be more. This is often true in many aspects of life, and is especially true with infographics.
- Know the value of white space. Content in your infographics will stand out and be clear if you get the spacing just right.
- Channel your inner designer. Get out of your comfort zone and try new things. The more you do it, the better you get in matching your message to your audience.

Top-Ten Infographic Elements

These are simple, yet powerful data-driven visual elements for your infographic. There are many types of visualizations that can highlight data. Table 5.1 includes my "Top Ten" approachable visualizations for use in infographics, in no particular order:

Table 5.1. Top Ten Infographic Elements

	Word cloud – A word cloud displays a set of words from a character data item. Depending on the type of word cloud and your data, the size and color of each word in the cloud can indicate the numeric data. These are great for highlighting importance and relative performance using words. Alternatively, a bubble plot could be used if words don't work for your design.
	Bar chart – A bar chart comprises vertical or horizontal bars that represent quantitative data. Use a small number of categories to best highlight comparative performance at a glance.
	Pie chart – Edward Tufte, an expert in visual communication of information, is not a supporter of the pie chart, and many others agree, but pie charts can be a useful and simple graph to show relative performance on a small number of categories. (Tufte, 2017)
	Key value or KPI gauge – Calling out important numbers is key. It is often useful to show a big number in your infographic. Percentages and big numbers are useful to show counts and amounts. Also, gauges are a great way to show actual versus target values.
	Correlation matrix or heat map – A correlation matrix displays the degree of correlation between multiple intersections of measures as a matrix. These are great to show relationships and highlight what matters from the data.
	Tables – A table displays data as text. The data should be ranked top or bottom, and five or fewer values is best. Sometimes, more data is needed to tell the story. However, brevity is key with this visualization.
	Line chart – A line chart shows the relationship of one or more measures over some interval, such as time or a series of ranges. Timelines are brought to life with this graph, and they are a relatable way to show data.

	Geo map – Geospatial data is a favorite of mine. It can take the digital world and overlay it on the physical world. Maps offer instant familiarity. Adding a geospatial element allows you to show data relationships using location which is powerful and intuitive when combined with other location data.
	Network – A network diagram consists of nodes (values) and links (relationships). It is a popular way to show relationships at a glance, which can reduce the time to achieve an insight.
	Treemap – A treemap displays a hierarchy or a category as a set of rectangular tiles. It is a great graph to show large amounts of data, multi-dimensional data (nested tiles), and multi-measure data (color and size).

Many more graph options are available depending on the story that needs to be told from the data. If you are like me, you might find one option that you use for a while, and then move onto another one, which might be more interesting to you and the audience.

Infographic Toolkit

It is sometimes hard to make a start with a task, but it is much easier when you have the tools to do what you need. Here is a checklist to get you started with your infographic:

- **A question to answer** – This is the fun part. What do you want to highlight to the audience?
- **Whiteboard or piece of paper** – These are used to get the ideas into the real world, and they are key tools in all information product design.
- **Data (the bigger, the better)** – There are more options for a story when you have more data. So, big data really is big opportunity when designing infographics. (Public data sources such as http://www.data.gov or http://www.open.canada.ca are good places to start. There are some great articles online that have done the hard work for you. Many articles provide links to particular open data).
- **Third-party graphics** – Like clip art is to typical business presentations, a good stock image and icon library is useful for infographics. Examples are at http://www.istockphoto.com, or free at http://www.freepik.com.
- **Color** – Get your color scheme organized early for less rework later. Some websites are really useful for generating compatible colors for use in your infographic. Two examples are Color Wheel (https://color.adobe.com/create/color-wheel) and Color Calculator (https://www.sessions.edu/color-calculator/).
- **Software** (in this case, SAS and Microsoft Office).

Chapter 6

Data to Insight

Overview

You might have read the title of this book and thought SAS is not a toolset for creating infographics. I would counter that SAS has been about creating information graphics to interpret data and information from the beginning and continues to provide context and enhance data to provide insight. This book is focused on a particular information product: the infographic.

Audience

This chapter has a little bit of everything for everyone. It discusses the roles and requirements for analytics and what SAS considers to be important considerations for true enterprise analytics.

The Challenge: From Data to Insight

Infographics are one way of communicating data through visualization. They are not the only information product that does a great job of highlighting the value of data. SAS has focused heavily on approachable ways to analyze data, to quickly focus on the value and to share insights.

The process to get the fastest insight from all available data requires us to understand the roles and requirements of all users in the organization to achieve the outcomes that are needed today and to provide a path for their use of data tomorrow and into the future. There is a growing need in organizations to enable all users to explore data and share insights when and if they require it. SAS has focused on all information users and is always trying to ensure that it provides the right tool for the right requirement.

The previous chapters contain ideas about creating infographics. So, let's now look a little closer at all information requirements and users in the enterprise. This chapter highlights the roles and requirements that users have in an organization and opens the conversation that more than just pretty pictures are needed to change behaviors and get competitive advantage.

Exploring the Requirements Continuum

Each user typically has an area of expertise within the requirements continuum. For example, consider the data scientist who works in finance, but does not have expertise in the sales domain. This type of user would need some guided entry points for areas in which they are not an expert although they can just access raw data within their focus domain.

The analytics platform should be flexible enough to cover all users' requirements in all scenarios, and not limit any user's potential. SAS enables all users to grow their skills inside an analytics platform that provides self-service software tools for all skills and requirements.

Figure 6.1 shows that analytics is a broad discipline and that all requirements need to be addressed.

Figure 6.1. Requirements Continuum

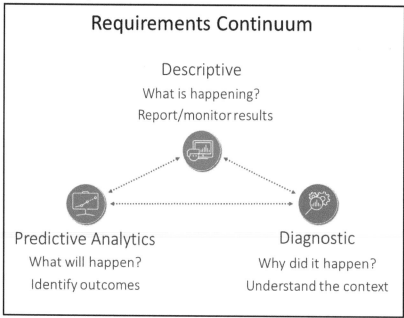

In a later chapter that shows scenarios in which infographics are developed, you will see a range of skills and tools that are covered to achieve a common goal: creating infographics with SAS. Requirements are broader than just infographics, and an analytics platform should assist an organization to address the requirements and user personas. Some analytics tools lack the coverage of features address these requirements and instead require the user to stitch together unrelated software to meet the complete requirement. SAS aims to address all requirements and user personas with a single, common platform.

Exploring the Roles Continuum

The roles that are held by people in an organization vary according to the jobs and skills that they have, as well as knowledge of data and internal processes.

Figure 6.2 shows the organization and its continuum of skills, including data science skills and more traditional business analysis skills.

Figure 6.2. Roles Continuum

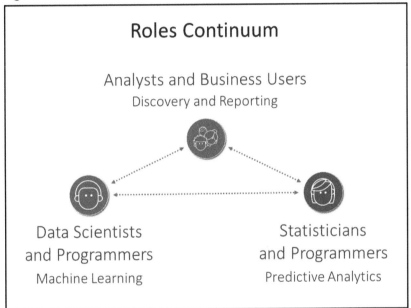

To get more value from your analytics investments, take a closer look at the people and their roles. For example, what are the needs of different types of users? What technological competencies are required from different types of roles, and what collaboration is required among different roles? What are the overlaps between different roles? In a modern organization, these skills can be categorized using the following roles:

Role: Analysts and Business Users

The business analyst understands the business context of underlying data and is focused on answering a defined question.

The person in this role provides guidance and support to stakeholders by building reports, dashboards and infographics, and by assisting in interpreting results.

What they need: Flexible, easy-to-use graphical user interfaces.

Role: Statisticians and Programmers

These users can be a blend of data scientist and business analyst who work with data preparation, exploration, and visualization.

The person in this role often explores the use of advanced analytic modeling techniques to solve a particular business problem using wizards and pre-built logic.

What they need: Flexible, easy-to-use graphical user interfaces. They also need some coding capability.

Role: Data Scientists and Programmers

The data scientist performs complex exploratory analysis, descriptive segmentation, and predictive modeling. The person in this role often investigates advanced analytic techniques and machine learning. The person in this role also identifies and prepares data needed for model development.

What they need: A choice of tools, advanced coding capability, and the ability to scale methods without redefining code.

These roles often act as creator of information products (like infographics) that are then consumed downstream: either by stakeholders, or by other systems as deployed analytical processes. It makes sense that popular infographics can also serve these multiple roles in your organization. The next part of the book discusses the platform needed to support these users.

The Platform – a Business Engine

Overview

This chapter provides an overview of what a platform to support all analytics users and requirements would look like. This is an outline only, and will illustrate functional components that are leveraged to achieve the end-to-end analytics workflow: the analytics life cycle. The ultimate goal of an analytics platform is to create the shortest path from data to decision, and this could be in the form of an infographic that is created from a vast volume of data in your organization.

Audience

All SAS users will get value from this section. It highlights how SAS is much broader than just the infographic.

SAS and the Analytics Lifecycle

If you bought this book, then you probably already know what SAS does. I will explain it quickly and you can either confirm your knowledge or pick up an additional piece of information.

SAS is the leader in advanced analytics. I could stop there, and it should then be very clear. However, I will drill down a bit further to explain what SAS does. As the market leader in analytics and data management, SAS has worked with customers to leverage data and analytics to impact business results. SAS is committed to helping organizations find critical answers to the biggest challenges. SAS customers are organizations large and small, including Fortune 500 companies, governments, nonprofit organizations, academia, small business, and even individuals.

Data is everywhere, but data alone has no value. To find the value and deeper understanding of data, there must be analytics. SAS knows that you and your organization want to find that deeper insight and do more than just solve basic problems. SAS is the engine to help you determine what's next.

SAS can embed intelligence into everything that an organization does, and can execute analytics wherever it is needed, whether on-site, in the cloud, or at the device. SAS can analyze any type of data. SAS provides an analytics platform that delivers business value and replaces confusion with clarity.

SAS is the proven engine to address the analytics lifecycle, which includes these phases: data, discovery and deployment. Figure 7.1 shows the analytics life cycle, which enables analytics as the core part of an organization's strategy:

Figure 7.1. Analytics Life Cycle (Image credit: S. Holder & T. Schweihofer, 2017)

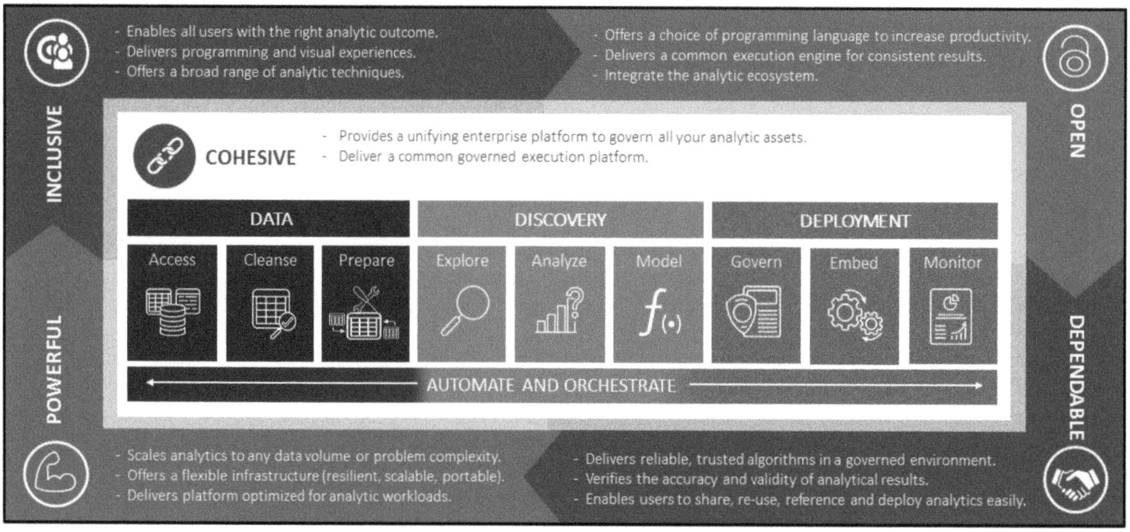

Data: Fuel for Decisions

Data holds the key for your organization to solve many problems or to create new business opportunities. But you must enable access to all available and relevant data. Unlike other vendors, SAS delivers cleansed, governed, real-time data from all your sources. This enables your analytics to perform across the entire organization.

Discovery: Make Data-Driven Decisions

Analysis is what enriches your data and gives context. You want a broad analytics toolbox with a deep and wide set of proven analytics capabilities for a wide variety of users. SAS provides a wide set of analytical capabilities: from statistics to machine learning and from cognitive programming in SAS to open-source languages for analytics.

Deployment: Drive the Business Where It Happens

Data and insight are worth very little if your organization can't make it a core part of business operations. SAS empowers you to integrate analytical results and insights back into your organization with speed and at scale, from the simple to the most complex operating environments.

SAS clearly solves more challenges for customers above and beyond creating business infographics, and for more information about this, see www.sas.com/customers. Visit the www.sas.com website to read more about what SAS customers are achieving with SAS and what can happen when you treat data and analytics as a strategic asset.

SAS Tools and Worked Examples

In **Part 2** we discuss the software used in this book and step through examples of creating Infographics with SAS. We demonstrate how to approach your projects all the way through to sharing your designs. You will be provided various software options to achieve infographic outputs in hope this will inspire you back in the office.

The Tools: Software Used in this Book

Overview

Even though the focus of this book is to create infographics with SAS, the tools we're covering, and SAS, more generally, has a much broader capability than what we use to achieve this focused task. This next section of the book aims to step you through the SAS products that we leverage in this book and to discuss their broader capability.

Audience

This is a general topic for all SAS users and will provide insight for all readers.

Tools Overview

There are many tools in the market to create and publish infographics as well as graphic designs, more generally. The focus is to show that SAS can be used to solve this business challenge. There is a rise in the market of providers trying to solve this data visualization challenge and to make it more approachable by removing the barrier to entry for business users and programmers. Many of these offerings require extensibility to solve for serious enterprise requirements. The power of the proven SAS platform is placed well to be extended to this business challenge. SAS is a proven and powerful tool that can be utilized to solve analytics problems and produce infographics without needing other software.

Here is an overview of selected SAS tools that can be used to produce the infographic examples that are outlined in this book. This is an overview of the SAS software components and a list of references to further enhance your learning. There are some great resources provided by SAS experts for each of these tools, and I have included some of these in the recommended reading listed in this book. The focus of this chapter is to ensure that functionality is understood, both to create the infographic and to understand the use cases beyond the infographics.

This section outlines the following tools from SAS:

- SAS Add-In for Microsoft Office (later used in Example 1 and 2)
- SAS Visual Analytics (later used in Examples 1, 2, and 3)
- SAS Studio (later used in Example 4)

SAS Add-In for Microsoft Office

Capability Overview

SAS Add-In for Microsoft Office is designed to enable users of Microsoft Office access to SAS analytics and visualization capabilities from within the Microsoft Office suite. SAS Add-In for Microsoft Office has been around for many years because SAS was early in determining the importance of bringing the analytics to the user rather than bringing the user to the analytics. SAS Add-In For Microsoft Office provides users with a customized ribbon inside the Microsoft Office products: Microsoft Word, Microsoft Excel, Microsoft PowerPoint and Microsoft Outlook. Here are the primary capabilities within SAS add-In for Microsoft Office:

- **Leverage SAS platform** – Add-In for Microsoft Office leverages the broader SAS platform, which includes functions like high-performance analytics and grid computing.

- **Familiarity** – Add-In for Microsoft Office provides a Microsoft Office user who uses familiar Windows desktop applications everyday with the exact same interface to access powerful features from SAS.

- **IT friendly** – Add-In for Microsoft Office connects using secure and auditable access to data and provides business users a great way to load spreadsheets and other business-specific content to the SAS enterprise analytics platform. This allows for reuse and sharing, which enables a true collaboration for business teams.

- **Guided analysis** – Add-In for Microsoft Office provides a simple wizard-driven. task-oriented user interface to enable a business user to get more than just data access. Users can apply analytics and create visualizations and reports from within Microsoft Office.

Figure 8.1 shows that every user gets the right interface when using SAS software.

Figure 8.1. Every User, Right Interface

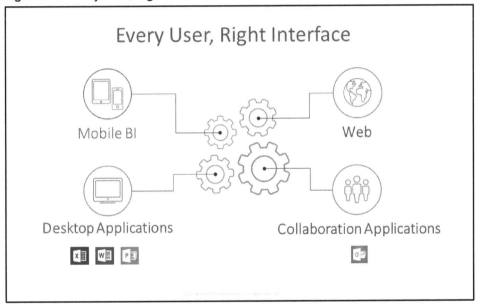

NOTE: SAS Visual Analytics Add-In for Office

A software bundle was released in 2016, SAS Visual Analytics Add-In for Office, which provides an abbreviated version of SAS Add-In for Microsoft Office. It includes a subset of features that focus on SAS Visual Analytics users. This version provides Excel and PowerPoint integration, but also removes more advanced features so that a business user can gradually step into more analytics features that are available in the complete SAS Add-In for Microsoft Office.

Typical Use Cases

In addition to creating business infographics with SAS and Microsoft Office, here are three use cases to show the value of using the SAS Add-In for Microsoft Office:

Use Case 1: The Presenter

The business user needs to embed one or more graphics elements from the SAS Visual Analytics dashboard or report. This user opens Microsoft PowerPoint and needs to present some company statistics to the boardroom each month. In the past, this user might have taken a screen capture and pasted the image into the presentation each month. However, this is very limited in management capability, not to mention understanding where the information ends up and if that information is secure.

This user can now open PowerPoint and insert a snapshot of year-to-date performance, which is automatically updated each month. A slide in the presentation needs to show only the business unit's performance and not show the company's overall performance. In this case the user can embed a filter to show only the business unit. Now the user is ready to present to the board meeting, not just today, but each month. This is due to the linkage between the presentation and the SAS analytics platform, which will now be refreshed each time the presentation deck is opened. Similar functions are highlighted in examples in the book, using Microsoft PowerPoint and SAS to create an infographic.

Use Case 2: The Spreadsheet Jockey

We all know people within our business who are the subject matter experts, they know all about the data and their business, and they are frequently asked by management to provide a view to support stakeholders and their business discussions. One problem with this type of approach is that the spreadsheet easily gets out of date. I've seen where a simple date filter written into a spreadsheet has turned a very serious discussion about performance into a data quality issue, which had been hidden by the spreadsheet's complexity. This user can still use the spreadsheet. However, now the user can drive elements of the data from other SAS assets that are defined in the platform. An example for this user is the ability to embed the data, which sits behind the same chart that is used by the preceding Use Case 1. The chart will stay linked to the original report and any subsequent functions and filters will flow through to the spreadsheet. Similar functions are highlighted in Example 2 later in the book, using Microsoft Excel and SAS to create a business infographic.

Use Case 3: "Regular Ad Hoc" Report Writer

In this use case, we see a business team that needs to provide the same highly formatted Word document each month and that needs a data-driven visual to embed into a handful of locations within the Word document. A customer once said to me that they do "regular ad hoc" reports, which is an interesting phrase, yet a common problem. Previously, this was not easy because, first, they had to find the data, and then they had to craft a visual or graphic representation for inclusion into the final document. This often meant that next month the whole process had to start over, wasting multiple people's time to validate an update on what were effectively the same elements with refreshed data. Using SAS Add-In for Microsoft Office and Microsoft Word, this team can now insert elements from multiple locations such as SAS Visual Analytics or custom visualizations using SAS tasks or even embed unique SAS stored processes to drive precise visuals. The benefits mean that this team needs only to open the document and refresh the content from SAS before sending the updated report to stakeholders. Savings in time alone make this use case a worthwhile activity. Figure 8.2 shows SAS Add-In for Microsoft Office within Microsoft Word which can help solve the regular reporting requirements.

Figure 8.2. SAS and Microsoft Word

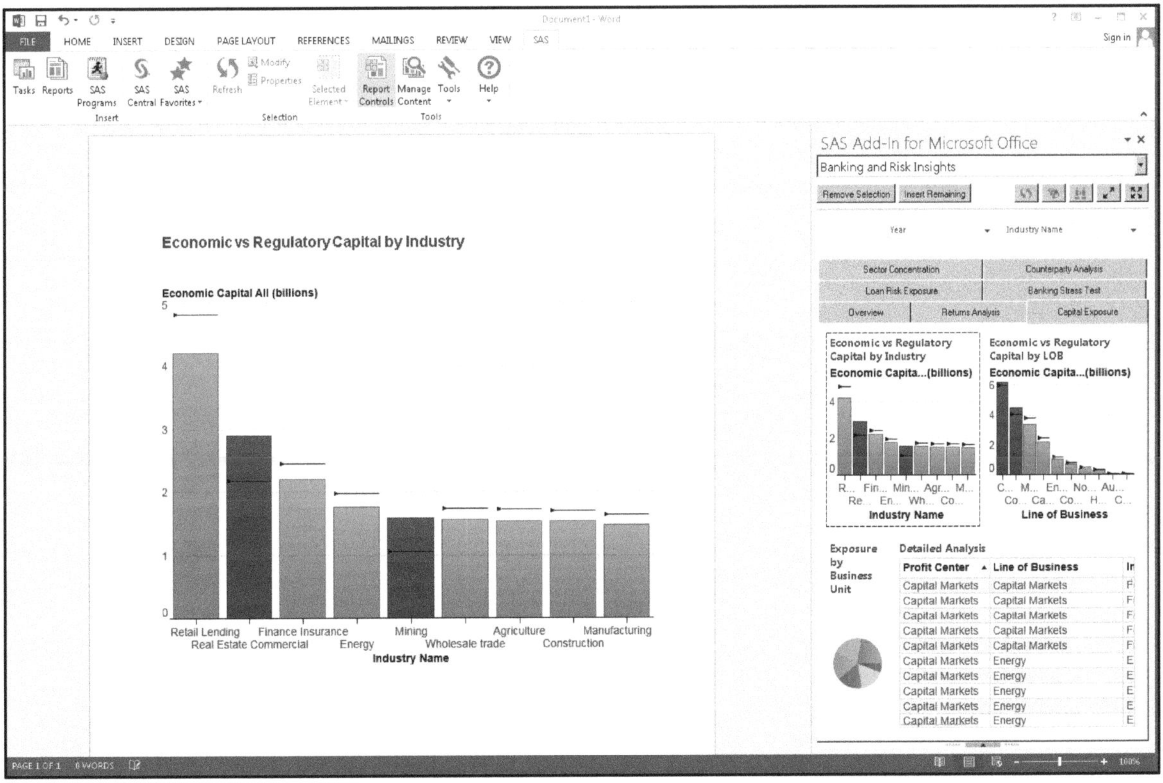

Tools Used

Tools used in this section are the SAS Add-In for Microsoft Office, which includes integration with Microsoft PowerPoint, Excel, Word, and Outlook. Examples in this book use SAS Add-In for Microsoft Office 7.15.

SAS Visual Analytics

Capability Overview

SAS Visual Analytics was designed to make data discovery and data visualization more approachable and to take analytics to a much broader audience. SAS released the SAS Visual Analytics suite to provide a much more user-friendly way to interact with big data. SAS Visual Analytics has provided access to the powerful SAS platform for a whole new set of users because no coding was required. This suite of visual products continues to develop, and the latest releases of SAS Visual Analytics include modules such as SAS Visual Statistics and SAS Visual Data Mining and Machine Learning, which use this same drag-and-drop approach as well as visualization to demystify analytics and statistics for a broader audience.

SAS tools have always been used to understand data and to surface patterns within the data. This traditionally was done by analysts and programmers who would write code that subsets the data and pull down what their computer could handle. Then, they would design their analysis on the sample of data that they could work with.

This time-consuming process was done only because the computation could not scale for the analyst. Today, with so much data, this approach was not sustainable.

SAS tools have been used for data discovery and deep exploration for many years. So, you might ask what is there to talk about here. The focus of this technology section is the self-service data exploration and deep exploration tools of SAS, SAS Visual Analytics, SAS Visual Statistics, and SAS Visual Data Mining and Machine Learning that access the high-performance analytic engine that runs on SAS Viya.

SAS Visual Analytics on SAS Viya was designed for a business user to perform self-service analysis and also to complement the broader analysis throughout the analytics lifecycle. From dashboards and reports to deep data exploration: SAS Visual Analytics is the solution to achieve self-service analytics.

Many people purchase SAS Visual Analytics for a particular use case. They have an immediate business problem and learn just enough to solve that need. In my experience, it is rare for a person to learn more about a software product than the initial demand. However, without a broader understanding of the capabilities of their software, when the next business challenge surfaces, the user might not know that SAS Visual Analytics could also be used to solve that next problem.

SAS Visual Analytics Capabilities

SAS Visual Analytics has a breadth of functionality that can be used to solve the following business tasks:

- **Visual data flow to conduct data preparation** – You can create data queries to perform joins, add calculated columns, transpose, subset and sort data, and load new data.

- **Reports and dashboards** – You can design reports once, and then distribute and publish anywhere (web, mobile, and Microsoft Office).

- **Interactive charts, visuals, and explorations** – You can discover insights from any size and type of data, from spreadsheets to Hadoop data, and all things in between.

- **Powerful, easy-to-use analytics** – You can use forecasting, goal seeking, scenario analysis, decision trees, path analysis. and other analytic visualizations. SAS Visual Analytics makes analytics approachable for the entire team. The machine-learning capability is enhanced further when adding SAS Visual Statistics and SAS Visual Data Mining and Machine Learning**.**

Figure 8.3 shows approachable analytics in one SAS solution.

Figure 8.3. SAS Visual Analytics Capability Overview

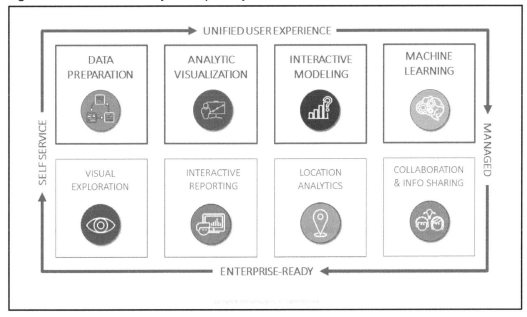

Typical Use Cases

Use cases for SAS Visual Analytics (SAS Visual Statistics and SAS Visual Data Mining and Machine Learning modules), are vast and varied. Here are a few use cases for which SAS Visual Analytics is used to solve business problems for customers.

Use Case 1: Approachable Analytics

Before looking to design an infographic or any information product, a user must first understand the data. One of the use cases for this toolset is for a business analyst to look at the data to understand the data and to clarify whether the data is useful to solving the business challenge. This use case identifies a subject matter expert in the data who can look into the data to see a clear picture of what is happening and to confirm or deny the assumptions that they have. Data analysis can be done using a highly visual user interface instead of understanding complex technology or coding to achieve the outcome.

Use Case 2: Deep Exploration

What fits nicely into the analytics life cycle is where the data scientist or traditional analyst uses a visual and a high performance toolset to achieve what would have taken much longer using traditional tools and methods. They can see all the data and quickly understand if the attributes in the data could assist with their models and further analysis.

Use Case 3: Dashboards and Reports

SAS Visual Analytics is great for easy-to-create and "accessible anywhere" dashboards for any business data. These dashboards are simple for a business analyst to create and share and collaborate with information consumers. The benefit here still remains the ability to embed highly visual, analytically powered elements to users who previously might never have seen these visuals as tools that they could use to tell a story with their data. Dashboards can also include infographic principles depending on your use case, as you will see in the worked examples in the following chapters.

Figure 8.4 shows simple, powerful, and flexible approachable analytics for all users.

Figure 8.4. SAS Visual Analytics Dashboard

> **NOTE: Skills Progression with SAS Visual Analytics**
>
> Analytics skills improvement is a by-product of deploying SAS Visual Analytics. A final example of where this process is useful is developing analytic skills within a business team. For example, a business team might not have the requisite skills to jump directly into analytics and would benefit from an easy-to-use toolset to start to understand how and where analytics will assist with their business challenges.

There are many more use cases for self-service data exploration and visualization with SAS Visual Analytics, and all business teams can benefit from these capabilities. Clearly, SAS Visual Analytics is much more powerful than just to assist in producing business infographics. SAS Visual Analytics is used in examples later in this book.

Tools Used

SAS has focused on developing data science skills in its customers, and, over recent years, with innovative self-service tools like SAS Visual Analytics and SAS Visual Statistics, SAS enables business analysts to gain skills toward data science. SAS provides the right tools for each person's skills, which means that each interface provides the right amount of functionality for any user's skill set, while providing a pathway to move forward once their skills develop.

- SAS Visual Analytics 8.2 on SAS Viya
- SAS Visual Statistics 8.2 on SAS Viya
- SAS Visual Data Mining and Machine Learning 8.2 on SAS Viya

SAS Code

Design Intent

When you use SAS software (listed in the preceding section), you will be executing commands generated using SAS code. SAS can be used to create business infographics. However, this is just the tip of the iceberg when talking about SAS capability. SAS code can perform an extensive range of tasks with regard to analytics, data management, and deployment.

At its core, SAS consists of code packages including Base SAS, which can be extended using various modules like SAS/STAT, SAS/GRAPH, SAS/OR, and SAS/ETS among others. Each module comes with SAS procedures to assist with specific functions. For example, SAS/GRAPH includes PROC GRADAR to create radar plots and to control all aspects of this process. SAS procedures include many options to be controlled by the analyst such as data, colors, visual display, and much more. This simple description only touches the surface of the capability of SAS. The main idea is that the SAS code modules are the engine room of SAS, and they are relied upon by customers across the globe to drive critical analysis and business solutions. This book is about visualizing data through infographics. Therefore, the focus is on SAS code to create infographics.

SAS has a component called SAS/GRAPH, which is the traditional graphing software module. SAS/GRAPH is a powerful data visualization tool that has been around for many releases of SAS and is still a very capable option for power users to visualize data. A newer graphing software option is an extension to SAS Output Display System (ODS), which can deliver content in almost unlimited ways. SAS ODS Graphics continues to be extended and is included within Base SAS and is used by the SAS procedures to generate graphics. It can be used directly with PROC SGPLOT and PROC SGRENDER.

In this book, SAS/GRAPH is mostly used to generate the coded infographic examples. However, you could achieve similar results if you used SAS ODS graphics. The goal of this book is to show examples of how SAS code can be used to create infographics, whichever component you choose to achieve this.

Figure 8.5 shows how SAS code can be used to visualize data.

Figure 8.5. SAS Code in SAS Studio

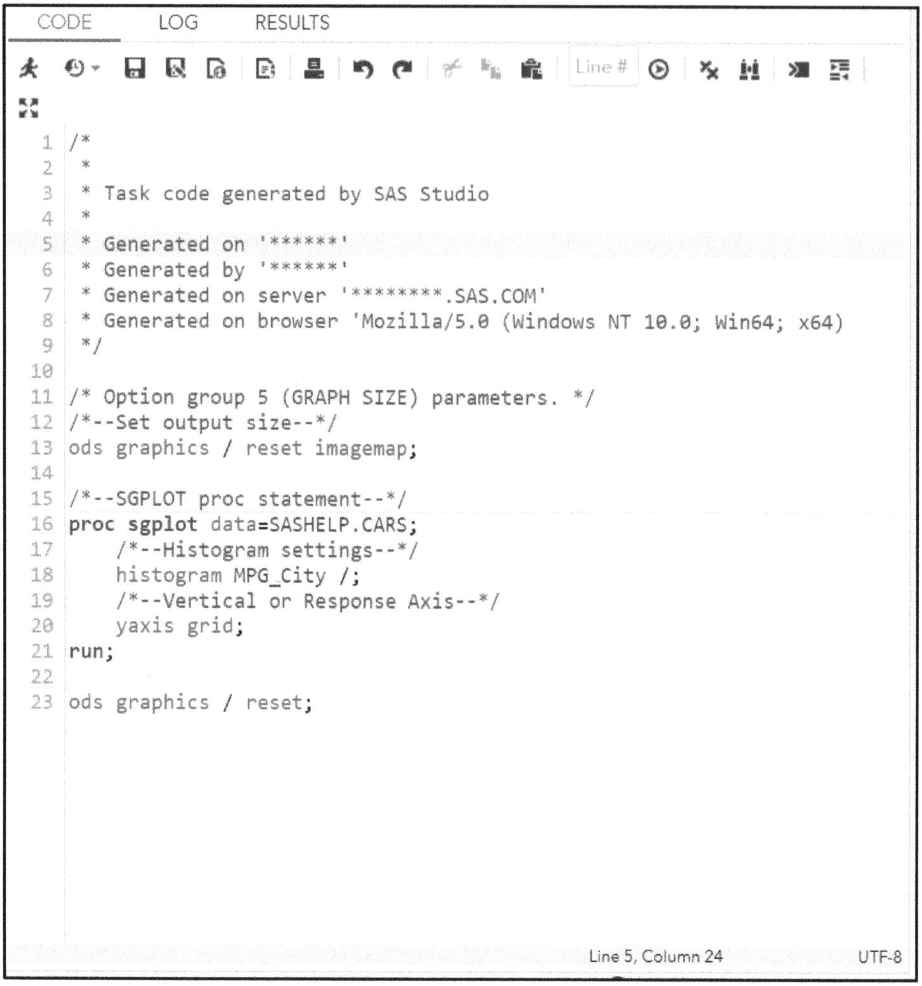

```
CODE        LOG        RESULTS

1   /*
2    *
3    * Task code generated by SAS Studio
4    *
5    * Generated on '******'
6    * Generated by '******'
7    * Generated on server '********.SAS.COM'
8    * Generated on browser 'Mozilla/5.0 (Windows NT 10.0; Win64; x64)
9    */
10
11  /* Option group 5 (GRAPH SIZE) parameters. */
12  /*--Set output size--*/
13  ods graphics / reset imagemap;
14
15  /*--SGPLOT proc statement--*/
16  proc sgplot data=SASHELP.CARS;
17      /*--Histogram settings--*/
18      histogram MPG_City /;
19      /*--Vertical or Response Axis--*/
20      yaxis grid;
21  run;
22
23  ods graphics / reset;
```

Line 5, Column 24   UTF-8

Typical Use Cases

Here are a few typical use cases for using SAS code to visualize data:

Use Case 1: Custom Designs

Customized and precise graphical output – Tell a story and control every element of the output with SAS code. Remember that with so much data out there today, you need powerful yet simple graphics to help the consumer understand the results.

Use Case 2: Templates

Leverage the Graph Template Language (GTL) – An extension to ODS, it enables you to create reusable graph templates that can be shared and are ready for the next data that you "throw" at them.

Use Case 3: Accessibility

Design data visualization with accessibility in mind – This is key to ensuring that all users can leverage your analysis. SAS graphics in combination with a SAS graphics accelerator – enable alternative presentations of SAS graphs for people who are visually impaired. SAS uses a combination of text and sonification (non-speech audio) to describe the data visualization to the end user to allow all users access to your graphics.

SAS code is used in examples later in this book.

Tools Used

SAS 9.4 M5 (including SAS/GRAPH software and SAS Output Delivery System)

> **NOTE: SAS Office Analytics**
>
> Base SAS, SAS/GRAPH, and SAS/STAT come as part of the SAS Office Analytics bundle, which is referenced throughout this book. This bundle includes SAS Add-In for Microsoft Office and SAS Enterprise Guide, among other software.

SAS Studio

Capability Overview

SAS Studio is a modern, unified graphical user interface (GUI) for use with the broader analytics platform. SAS has made SAS software available to all students around the world and provides SAS Studio as the GUI to learn SAS.

Many people write programs in SAS by using an application on their PC desktop or SAS server. SAS Studio is similar. However, it is a tool that you can use to write and run SAS code through your web browser. With SAS Studio, you can access your data files, libraries, and existing programs, and you can write new programs. When you use SAS Studio, you are also using SAS software, "behind-the-scenes." SAS Studio connects to a SAS server in order to process SAS commands. The SAS server can be a hosted server in a cloud environment, a server in your local environment, or a copy of SAS on your local computer.

After the code is processed, the results are returned to SAS Studio.

Figure 8.6 shows the ease of self-service graphics and custom-coded graphics.

Figure 8.6. SAS Studio

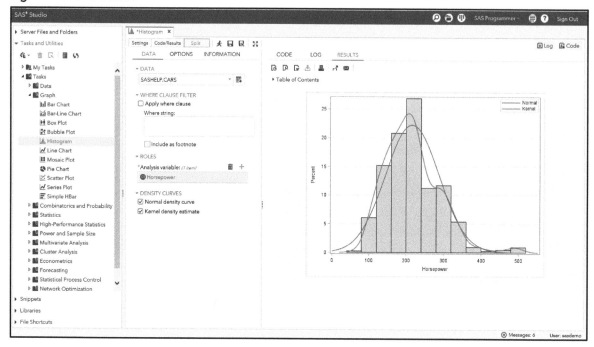

Some people originally thought SAS Studio was only a code editor that was similar to the SAS windowing environment, which is the programmer's interface, and this was probably true at some point. However, SAS Studio goes well beyond that initial goal. It is a "use anywhere" on any device development environment for SAS users. It is a web browser-based, SAS development toolset, which includes an assistive framework that uses built-in tasks and configurable, user-defined tasks to ensure a quick start for which repeatable benefit is gained for the analyst. This enables analysts to get their SAS tasks done faster. This offering sits somewhere in between SAS Enterprise Guide and the SAS windowing environment when comparing functionality. Like all great software, SAS Studio has overachieved from a simple vision and includes a visual code workflow mode and a power user's code mode to cover many preferences and many use cases.

This product is so important to SAS that it now fronts our next-generation offerings of SAS Viya and our SAS Learning Edition, which has had over half a million downloads since its release and continues to grow. SAS Studio is fast becoming the preferred interface of the next generation of SAS analysts and data scientists. Here are some features that assist users in taking advantage of their SAS investment as well as developing their skills in data science:

- **Assistive task framework** – Create reusable and shared tasks to grow the broader team's skills and share best practices.

- **Programming interface** – A web browser-based coding interface that is modern and simple.

- **Table viewer and automated query options** – A simple way to look at data.

- **Visual workflow** – Easy-to-use visual flows to understand each step in the analysis.

- **Security and auditability** – Enterprise grade software for IT teams.

- **User-specific preferences** – Remembers the user's preferences, even though you are using a web browser.
- **Automated code prompting and in-context help options** – Includes all the user needs to understand the procedures and options without leaving the code.

There are many more capabilities and more are added to each release of SAS Studio.

Typical Use Cases

In Chapter 13, you will see examples of infographics that were created with SAS code and that is submitted using SAS Studio. However, here are three more use cases to show where SAS Studio could be useful in your day job.

Use Case 1: Sitting on the Beach

If your idea of fun is sitting poolside or surfside and logging on to work on your mobile device, tablet. or wafer-thin, super-expensive laptop, to run some SAS jobs, then SAS Studio is for you! By accessing SAS on your web browser, a SAS analyst is now ready to work anywhere, anytime.

Use Case 2: Drive Reuse and Collaboration

SAS Studio enables you to create a pool of analytics assets for your broader analytics team to leverage. This use case highlights the ability for a group of users to access out-of-the-box, ready-to-fill-in the prompts, self-service analytics. This gives the analyst a bit of help while still giving access to the code to try other options in their analysis.

Use Case 3: Explore Data in a Simple Way

SAS Studio enables access for an analyst to view the data in a table, or even generate data if they have the permission to do so. This means that analysts can use the SAS platform to access and generate queries to understand the data and decide what the data could offer.

NOTE: SAS Enterprise Guide

SAS has other client software to execute SAS such as SAS Enterprise Guide, which continues to be popular for many SAS customers. It is not covered in the book. However, many books and blogs have been written to show how SAS Enterprise Guide helps analysts deliver value from their data.

SAS Studio is used to execute the SAS code and return the outputs for some examples in this book.

Tools Used

SAS Studio

Worked Examples

Overview

This chapter introduces worked examples of the approaches to create infographics with SAS. It contains step-by-step procedures to produce sample infographics with SAS. This section uses the Add-In for Microsoft Office with SAS, SAS Visual Analytics, and SAS code to design and create the infographics. All files are available for you to step yourself through these scenarios on your own time.

This part of the book is where you get your hands on the tools, and you start to build the examples that can help with your own data in your work environment. You will be leveraging the software outlined in the previous chapter to create a combination of data-driven graphics in the SAS software tools and subjective content and building an infographic template inside SAS Visual Analytics, Microsoft PowerPoint, and Microsoft Excel. The first examples require no coding skills at all, and are the most approachable options to help get you started today.

To use any of these examples, you need to do some work inside SAS Visual Analytics first to create the data-driven objects. Of course, you could just open a favorite SAS Visual Analytics report and use any object that other users in the organization have created for you. You will use some existing graphs from existing SAS reports, and you will later create your own graphs in SAS Visual Analytics.

Audience

All SAS users will be provided with options and examples in this chapter. You will move through basic, intermediate, and advanced SAS skills with each example. There is something for everyone in the following worked examples.

Sample Files

Sample SAS files are provided for reference along with the data and image files needed to reproduce these examples.

All files are provided for download here:

http://support.sas.com/murphy

NOTE: Sample Data

In the book, the sales data is focused on a fictitious toy company utilizing sample data shipped with SAS Visual Analytics. This focus enables you to maximize your efforts as you consider the visual elements of your infographics. Also, many organizations are driven by metrics such as profit, revenue, and costs, which makes this use case broad for many readers.

This data choice might make some readers sigh, thinking "more fake sales data for some made-up company!" You are being heard, loud and clear. The reason to choose and stick with a simple and familiar SAS data set is that this book aims to show you a repeatable approach to your own data. The more familiar you become with the approach and the simpler it is to try for yourself, the more likely you will learn from the examples. Familiarity with the data also helps people in all stages of their SAS skills journey.

I hope you see the benefits of using a simple data set throughout this book. The book is about what is possible with your data, not the data itself. Based on your feedback, I will be open to include more data in future updates of this book, especially because the sample data that ships with SAS also evolves over software releases.

Please refer to Appendix A for a complete overview of the Sample Data and the preparation steps to get ready for these examples.

Creative Content

Prior to beginning the work on your infographic, you need to ensure that you have all images and creative content for the infographic. This includes images for backgrounds and non-data-driven visuals, such as logos and layout graphics. At this point, consider fonts that best reflect the look that you are after. Selection of your graphical and typographical elements in advance will save you a huge amount of time. These assets are your infographic toolkit, and are the building blocks for your design.

Tools

The following tools are required to start the process to create an infographic:

- **Writing apparatus** – Whiteboard or pen and paper.
- **SAS software and Microsoft Office software** – Check the Tools Used sections in Chapter 8 for more.
- **Enthusiasm and patience** – The trial-and-error approach can be frustrating until you get the hang of it all.

Ready, Set, Go!

Let's look at the SAS tools outlined in Chapter 8 and show by example, step-by-step, how you can create and emulate some examples using SAS and Microsoft Office.

Here are the tools to be used in the examples following this chapter:

- SAS and Microsoft PowerPoint
- SAS and Microsoft Excel
- SAS Visual Analytics
- SAS code

Chapter 10

Example 1: SAS and Microsoft PowerPoint

Overview

This example provides a worked solution with zero code by using the drag-and-drop interfaces of SAS Visual Analytics and SAS Add-In for Microsoft Office. This worked example uses SAS Visual Analytics dashboards and insights. I will import elements of an existing dashboard and a report into an infographic created in Microsoft PowerPoint. Business analysts are very familiar with Microsoft PowerPoint and will be extending their use of this familiar toolset with content from SAS.

The general premise of designing infographics with SAS is that we are looking to create repeatable and robust infographics that are suitable for business use, compared to those not created in SAS which, while beautiful, may not provide the repeatable and simple access to corporate data.

Audience

This example can be skipped if the user is advanced. However, this user might find that the business interfaces and easy drag-and-drop approach are interesting if they know only the coded interface. This example is designed for a business user, a novice SAS user, or an intermediate SAS user.

Sample Files

Completed SAS Visual Analytics report examples and templates in PPTX format and completed infographics in PPTX format are provided for reference along with the data and image files needed to reproduce these examples.

All files are provided for download here: http://support.sas.com/murphy

Getting Started with SAS and Microsoft Office

For this example you will want some of your infographic content to be entered as subjective comments, with third-party graphics, and other content imported easily from SAS Visual Analytics. This option enables you to leverage the large investment in data assets in your enterprise, as well as provide the creative freedom that you need to create the narrative required to communicate the insight in the "eight-second window."

This option uses approachable analytics tools, SAS Visual Analytics and your Microsoft Office tools to make it accessible by any business analyst or report user. This option can unlock big data analytics into the infographics created by business analysts.

Step Zero: Start with a Mockup Design

To simplify this example, we will use a template as a starting point. I already know by looking at the template what is required for design and subject matter.

If you want to save time in any infographic creation process, you should start with a whiteboard or piece of paper and get it all out of your head and into the world. This step should provide ideas for topic, context, questions you want to answer or highlight, and design ideas. You will see this message throughout the book, and is guaranteed to provide you with a better infographic and to save you plenty of time. The mockup for Example 1 is shown in Figure 10.1.

Figure 10.1. Whiteboard Mockup for Infographic Design

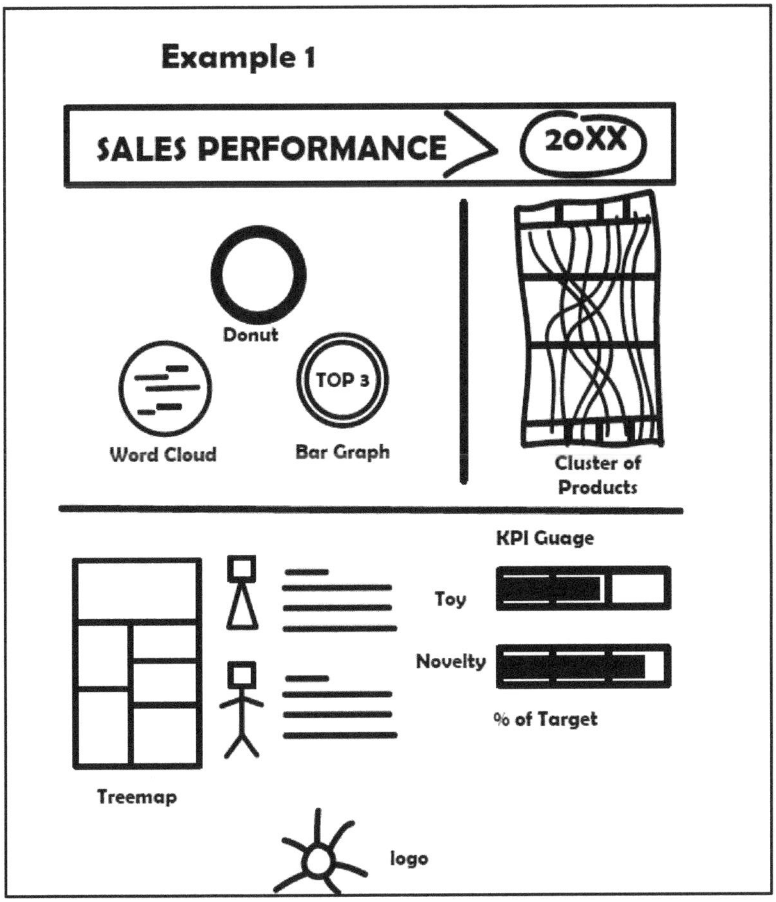

Step 1: Open the Template in PowerPoint

Open the example file Example_1_Template.pptx from your sample files to get started with the activity.

Figure 10.2 shows template, which contains a selection of images and clipart that are ready to use in the infographic.

Figure 10.2. PowerPoint Template

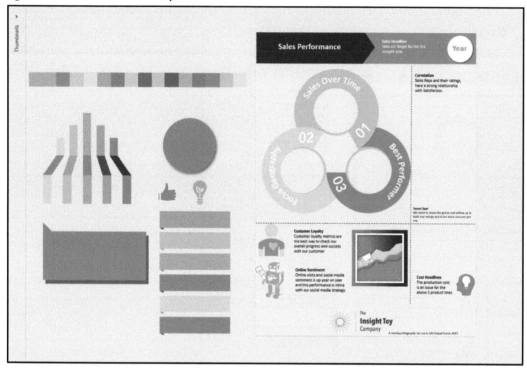

Inside this PowerPoint template are some important elements. There are some clipart-style images and icons, a color palette, some text, and a layout that is already displayed. By using this template, you are not starting from a blank canvas and you get some understanding of the context and design already by using this template.

The template has a custom slide size that is defined in PowerPoint and that allows for enough space to create the infographic with correct ratios. You can create your own slide very quickly by copying this custom slide.

Step 2: Connecting to SAS Visual Analytics

To connect to SAS, select the **SAS** tab from the Microsoft PowerPoint ribbon, as seen in Figure 10.3.

Figure 10.3. SAS Add-In for Microsoft Office ribbon

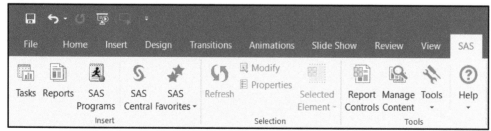

From Microsoft PowerPoint, select the **Tools** tab and the **Connections** option to connect to the SAS Visual Analytics server (see Figure 10.4).

Figure 10.4. SAS and Microsoft PowerPoint - Connections

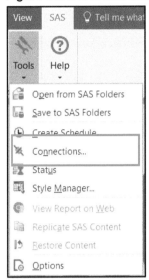

The user is presented with a window that includes options to add a new SAS server or to connect to an existing SAS server (Figure 10.5).

Figure 10.5. SAS and Microsoft PowerPoint Connections window

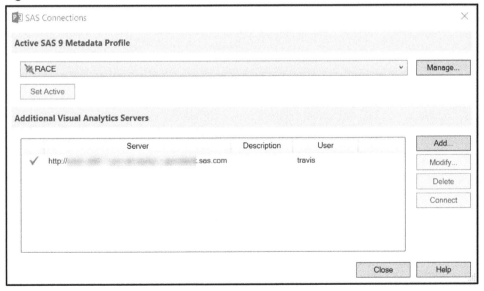

Setting up the connections is a one-time task. Connections setup will provide the user with access to the SAS servers from which to access reports, analysis, and functions that will allow content to be included in their Microsoft Office document.

Step 3: Deciding What Content to Leverage from SAS

This example assumes that some SAS Visual Analytics reports and analysis have been created already by someone in your organization. This means you don't have to leave Microsoft PowerPoint at all. If you do not have the SAS Visual Analytics reports, then this would be an additional step here. Please see other examples in Chapter 12 to see how to create SAS Visual Analytics reports and dashboards.

In this example, you already have two reports created using SAS Visual Analytics. The first report is a dashboard for a sales team, and the second is an ad hoc analysis created by the business analyst in the sales operations team. Both reports add value to your understanding of the sales performance at the Insight Toy Company.

Report 1: The Sales Performance Dashboard

Figure 10.6 shows elements from a report that are interesting and that would enhance the infographic.

Figure 10.6. Sales Performance Dashboard

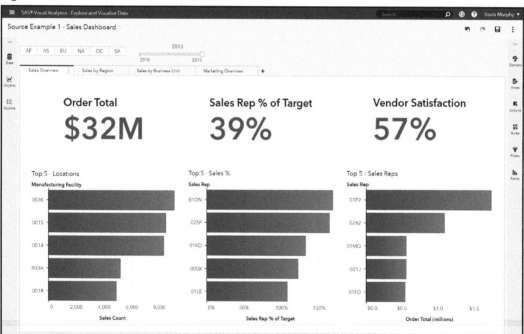

The infographic could contain a Top 5 performers bar chart, a word cloud of what is being sold, and a treemap (tile chart) of products for sale. A key performance indicator or gauge could also be useful at calling out performance. A geomap can also be a powerful visual from a traditional dashboard and in an infographic style dashboard.

Next, think about which of these elements will help to tell your story about sales performance. Do not include the elements that distract from this message.

Report 2: Ad Hoc Analysis on Sales Performance

Figure 10.7 shows the elements of the ad hoc analysis, which include a correlation matrix, a parallel coordinates plot, a forecast of sales overtime, and a network diagram about the relationship of products to product lines.

Figure 10.7. Ad Hoc Sales Data Exploration

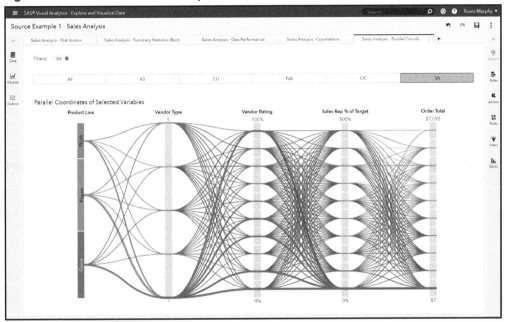

Once again, from these elements, you will select the ones that assist in telling the story that you want to tell in your infographic.

Step 4: Unifying the Content Elements

It is now time to unify these visual elements into the infographic itself. If you are like me, you can spend a long time getting your visual elements just right. Many iterations of design and trial-and-error will probably occur before you have the desired layout and information to tell the narrative that you want from your data.

Figure 10.8 shows how you can navigate to all your SAS Visual Analytics reports and analysis, and insert the desired elements into your infographic.

Figure 10.8. SAS and Microsoft PowerPoint: Navigation to Reports Using SAS Add-In for Microsoft Office

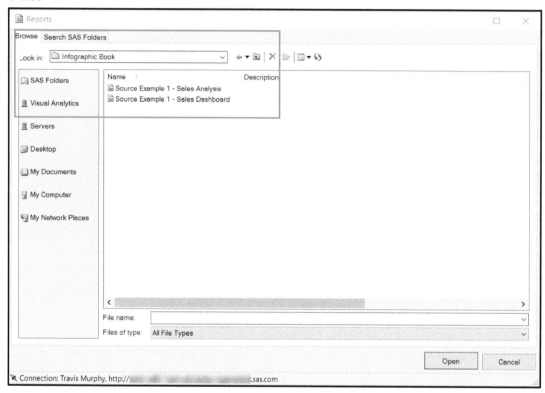

Adding content from SAS Visual Analytics is very easy, and don't forget that the computation is happening on the SAS platform, not on your computer.

After we select the appropriate content, we will select a report and click the **Open** button.

Repeat the preceding steps to add a second report, which is the ad hoc exploration report. This report has some additional options for use in this infographic. The approachable analytics will make a big impact to your audience.

Once you have selected one or more reports to open in Microsoft PowerPoint, you are presented with a preview window that shows the report contents. This is a live view of the report, and shows you the latest data that is loaded into SAS (see Figure 10.9).

Figure 10.9. SAS Add-In for Microsoft Office Report Controls Dialog

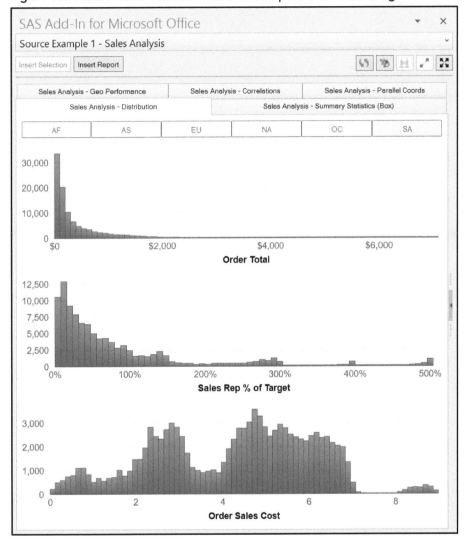

The preceding figure shows the live preview dialog for the SAS report. You can select the report that you want to work with if you have multiple reports open within the same Microsoft Office document. Your selected report shows a preview of all available elements to use in your document.

Step 5: Adding Elements to the Microsoft PowerPoint Document

To add an element to the Microsoft PowerPoint document right-click the element and select **Insert.** The element will now be added to the document.

From the Sales Dashboard: Report 1 Elements

Repeat the preceding steps to insert the following elements:

- **Dynamic Text Object** – Dynamic text can be added from the SAS Visual Analytics report to show a dynamic Year to facilitate easier updates in the future.

- **Key Value Object – Order Total** can be added as a single number that is aggregated in the infographic.

- **KPI Gauge Object – Sales by Product Brand** can be added as a clear measure of performance at a high level for each key product brand.

- **Word Cloud Object – Sales by Country for Selected Continent** can be added using a word cloud to show the best sales across the focus region.

- **Bar Graph – Top Product Sales by Product Line** can be added to show the bestselling product lines for the selected region.

- **Treemap Object** – The treemap can be added to show loyalty programs for customers in selected region.

Note these objects are filtered by our selections in the SAS Visual Analytics report. In this example, you are filtering on "South America." You make selections with the report controls dialog and filter selections in the report preview. This context can be saved with the document, and the context can be cleared at any time.

From the Data Exploration: Report 2 Element

Repeat the process to insert the second report for **Parallel Coordinates Graph** which can be added to show factors of each product line that is sold for the South America region of our toy company. The parallel coordinates plot can show the pattern of what our customers are buying. As you can see in Figure 10.10, the SAS content has been included in the Microsoft PowerPoint document while maintaining a link to SAS Visual Analytics. The document can be edited for a better fit in the infographic design.

Figure 10.10. Elements Added to Microsoft PowerPoint

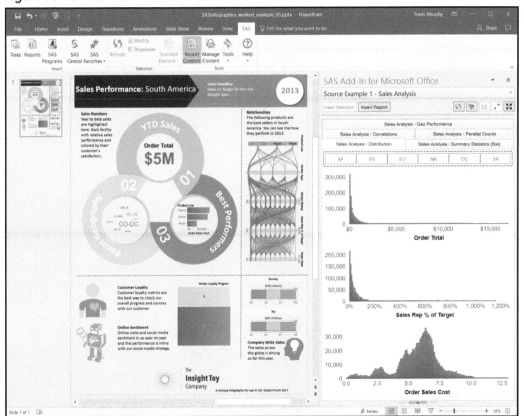

Step 6: The Final Touches

Now the data has been included in the infographic, some formatting and updates to the text headings and comments might be required. These subjective steps will add the final touches to the infographic in order to tell the story that you want. Use this step to confirm that the context is clear for the intended audience of the infographic, and that you have enough headings and commentary. Here are a few examples of final touches:

- **Text** – Add subjective context and clear linkage between the visuals and the story.

- **Placement** – Alignment, spacing, and scale are key to getting the infographic just right.

- **Colors** – SAS objects are being displayed as the SAS Visual Analytics report was set. These can be changed in SAS and automatically refreshed in PowerPoint. Other colors for background and text within PowerPoint are worth revisiting here.

Step 7: Share the Infographic

When you are happy with the final touches, you should save the output. Instead of selecting the standard document type (PPTX format), you can choose either the PNG format or PDF format to save the entire infographic that is ready for sharing. Figure 10.11 shows the final infographic.

Figure 10.11. Completed Infographic Created with SAS and Microsoft PowerPoint

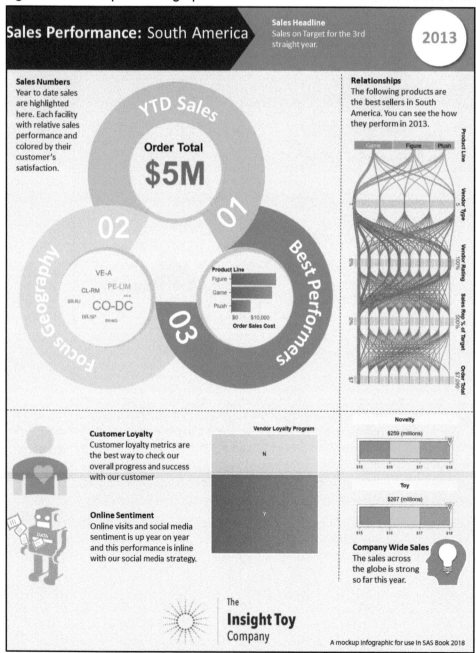

This infographic contains visual objects that are driven by the SAS analytics platform. It is considered to be highly credible for the boardroom because trusted data sources are used to drive the visual elements.

Why Use this Approach?

Here are a few benefits of using SAS and Microsoft Office:

- **Repeatable** – You can refresh each visual at the preferred interval (weekly or monthly, as you wish). You can leverage up-to-date SAS data via the **SAS** tab from the Microsoft Office ribbon.

- **Scalable** – You can scale to massive amounts of data, enabling the computational power of the SAS analytic engine to be leveraged beneath what seems to be a simple summary.

- **Approachable** – No coding is required! This approach leverages skills that a novice SAS user already has, including competency with Microsoft Office, the SAS drag-and-drop user interface, and SAS Visual Analytics. Advanced SAS users can do more in Microsoft Office with SAS code, which is covered in chapter 11.

Examples Gallery

Using Example 1 as a model, Figures 10.12–10.14 give additional examples of infographics that use SAS and Microsoft PowerPoint.

Figure 10.12. Example 1: Using SAS and Microsoft PowerPoint

Figure 10.13. Example 2: Using SAS and Microsoft PowerPoint

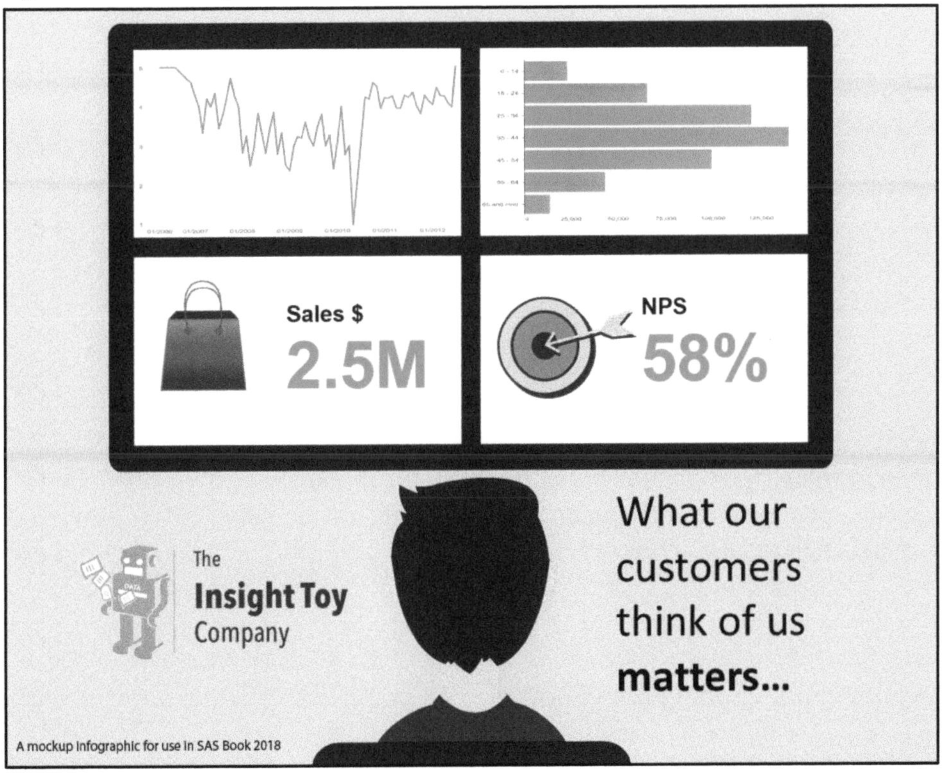

Figure 10.14. Example 3: Using SAS and Microsoft PowerPoint

Example 2: SAS and Microsoft Excel

Overview

Example 2 is aimed at the spreadsheet user, and includes additional options for a traditional Microsoft Office user beyond what is available in Example 1. Microsoft Excel is a popular software that is used by many organizations.

In this example, we are using both the simple drag-and-drop approach and a SAS code sample. This approach enables members of the team with different skill sets to be part of a broader infographic project. This example uses some SAS pre-built code and includes some SAS Visual Analytics elements. It also leverages SAS Add-In for Microsoft Office with Microsoft Excel.

Audience

All SAS users are covered in this chapter because we use simple, intermediate and some advanced elements of the SAS software.

Sample Files

Completed source SAS Visual Analytics report examples and templates in XLSX format, completed infographics in XLSX format, and SAS code are provided for reference along with the data and image files that are needed to reproduce these examples.

All files are provided for download here:

http://support.sas.com/murphy

Enhance with Analytics

Example 2 targets a more advanced SAS user who leverages more advanced analytics and visualizations for the infographic but who also uses a drag-and-drop interface. This example leverages the SAS stored process, which allows a more advanced user to focus on elements that are not typically performed by the business user. This approach removes limitations that might have existed in the first example because the data analyst with deeper skills in a particular analytics discipline is able to create a custom graphic by leveraging the powerful code base of SAS. There are also drag-and-drop options that are available for an intermediate user to also start down this path using tools such as SAS Studio and SAS Enterprise Guide to create task-driven, yet configurable and powerful reusable data visualizations.

This example shows that you are not limited to using SAS Visual Analytics reports only and demonstrates specific features of the SAS engine. This example starts to bring the data science team into your general business operations with your traditional business intelligence teams. Or, even your line of business can focus on what they're good at and still stepping up and asking for a little bit extra help from the data science unit.

This example enables you to leverage some pre-built, yet custom, analytics from SAS to embed elements into your infographics. You will leverage custom code and a SAS stored process from your data science team and create a linked process to run each month, quarter, or week as required. This means you are not limited to using just the predefined SAS Visual Analytics reports, but can include some custom SAS stored process and insert an element of your infographics that is driven by custom analysis, right next to objects inserted via a simple drag-and-drop method using approachable analytics tools such as SAS Visual Analytics.

This example provides a great way of adding some additional power into your infographics and still maintaining governance and a simple and maintainable framework to repeat and update your infographics into the future.

Step Zero: Create a Strawman Design for the Infographic

I have mentioned this a few times in the book, but if you want to save time in any infographic process, you should start with a whiteboard or piece of paper, and get it all out of your head and into the world. This step should provide ideas for topic, context, questions you want to answer or highlight, and design ideas. You are also not inhibited or constrained at this point, and I find that you can innovate within this early stage better and more easily than if you are at the computer.

Figure 11.1 is an example of a strawman design:

Figure 11.1. Strawman of Infographic Layout

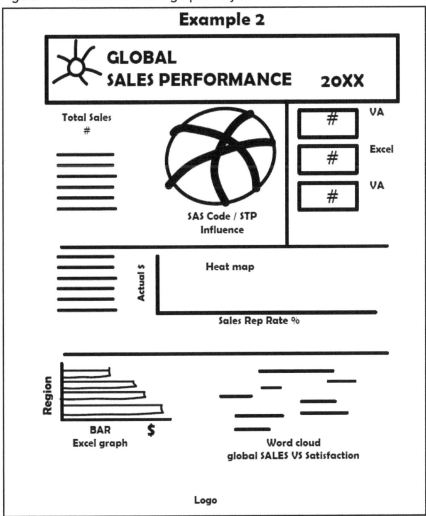

Step 1: Using SAS and Microsoft Excel

We are opening a predefined template in XLSX format, which has some settings that are configured for a printable and shareable infographic. This is done using options to manage the print area, page break definitions, and objects included as text boxes for easier formatting in Microsoft Excel.

Using your PC, open Microsoft Excel using your icon in your programs menu.

The Example2_Template_Start.xlsx file will already have some content placeholders and some icons and images included to give the start you need to progress in the steps to follow.

Step 2: Working with SAS Visual Analytics Report and Microsoft Excel

Connect to the SAS server, and open a SAS Visual Analytics report as we did in Example 1, Step 1. However, this time we will open Example 2 - Sales Report from SAS and navigate to your SAS Visual Analytics report. See Figure 11.2 for how to open a report.

Figure 11.2. SAS and Microsoft Excel: Opening a SAS Report using the SAS ribbon in Microsoft Excel

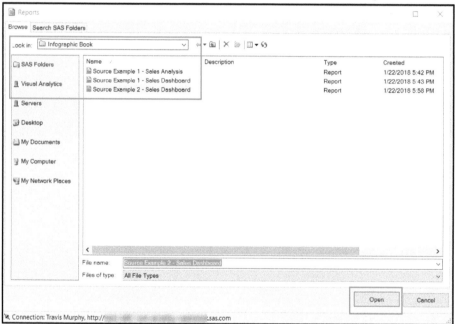

The report will open in Microsoft Excel. This should look familiar as the SAS Add-In for Microsoft Office is consistent across all Microsoft Office tools to make it easy for a user to use skills in SAS regardless of how they access it.

Step 2a: Insert the Heatmap

Using the SAS report controls dialog, you can explore and navigate to the reports to see what is useful for your infographic. In the main tab of the workbook, insert the heatmap object from your Visual Analytics report tab named **Sales Vs Customer Satisfaction**, as seen in Figure 11.3.

Figure 11.3. SAS and Microsoft Excel: SAS Visual Analytics report in Microsoft Excel

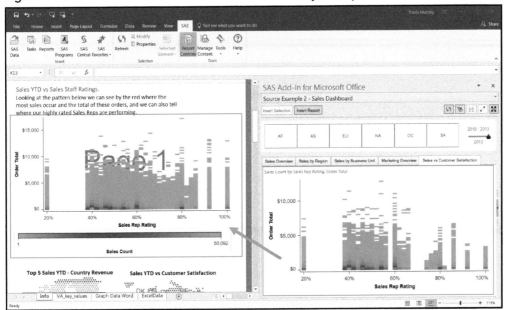

By inserting the element in this tab, we can use the graph in our design just as it comes out of SAS Visual Analytics. This is done by selecting a cell inside your design and inserting the SAS Visual Analytics heatmap. The heatmap now appears inside our Microsoft Excel infographic. You can also reposition this element to the desired size and layout in your design.

Step 2b: Insert the Word Cloud

Using the SAS report controls dialog again, you can navigate to the report sections to see what else is useful for your infographic, as seen in Figure 11.4.

Figure 11.4. SAS and Microsoft Excel: Inserting the Word Cloud Report Element from SAS Visual Analytics into Microsoft Excel

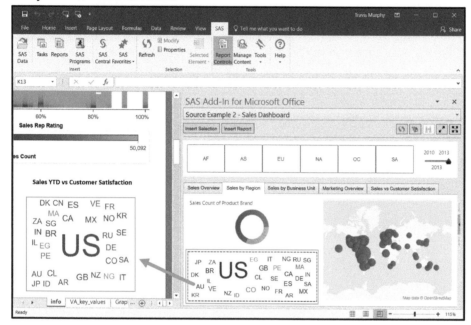

Although the word cloud is a great visual for an infographic, in this example I am going to use the data derived from this element in a standard Excel chart: the bar chart. This means I can use SAS Visual Analytics to provide Microsoft Excel the data from SAS Viya, yet still use the familiar Excel charts that I want to include in my design. In Figure 11.5, we can see the option to extract (or remove) data from the selected element.

Figure 11.5. SAS and Microsoft Excel: Extract Graph Data Option in SAS Add-In for Microsoft Office

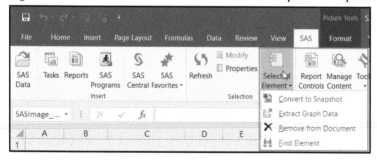

Figure 11.6. Microsoft Excel with SAS – Extracted Graph Data inserted into Microsoft Excel

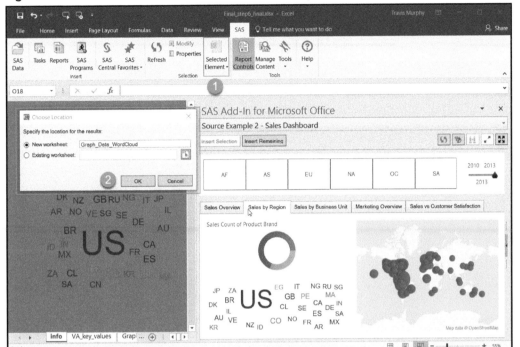

The extracted data can be placed in the same worksheet in Microsoft Excel or in a new worksheet by following the numbered actions in Figure 11.6. An important note here is that the data is still connected to SAS Visual Analytics on SAS Viya. Therefore, you can change the filters in the SAS Visual Analytics report and the data is updated. Whatever happens to the word cloud graph will also apply to the extracted graph data. You can disconnect the data if you desire. However, this is a powerful feature for reuse and scale to stay connected to your analytics platform. You can see the result of your export in Figure 11.7.

Figure 11.7. SAS and Microsoft Excel: Data Extracted from the SAS Visual Analytics Word Cloud and inserted into Excel.

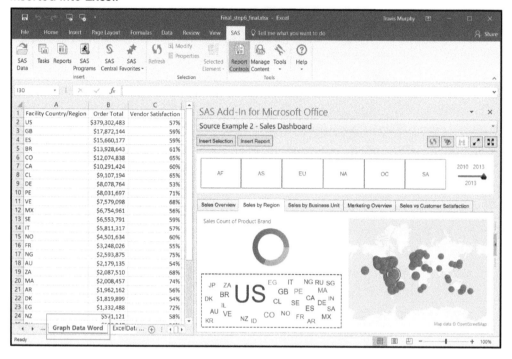

It is now time to insert the Excel bar chart, and once this is in place, you can edit the source data, as seen in Figure 11.8.

Figure 11.8. SAS and Microsoft Excel: Using standard Microsoft Excel Menus to Assign Extracted SAS Data to the Microsoft Excel Graph

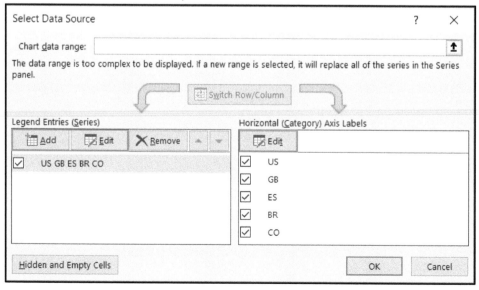

The following two actions just add some extra Microsoft Excel formatting and sorting to the graph, as follows. First, set the background to an image from our clipboard (using image person.png from the samples) as seen in Figure 11.9:

Figure 11.9. SAS and Microsoft Excel: Excel properties used to format data sourced from SAS Visual Analytics

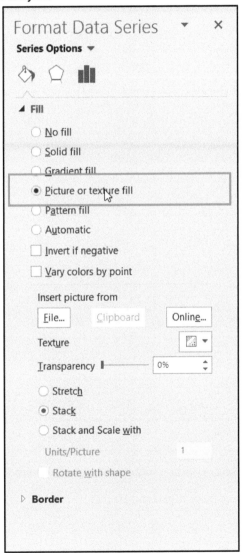

Then, set the sort order for the Excel bar chart as seen in Figure 11.10:

11.10. SAS and Microsoft Excel: Excel Properties Used to Sort Data from SAS Visual Analytics

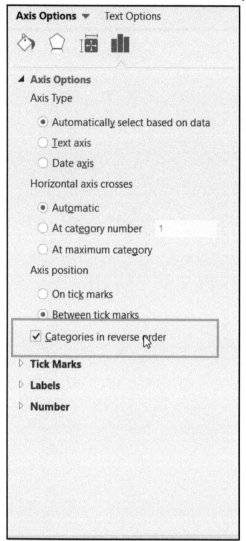

You could continue to configure the Excel graph if you think you need more formatting applied.

Figure 11.11 shows the final bar chart graph that is using SAS linked data, and a native Microsoft Excel chart.

Figure 11.11. SAS and Microsoft Excel: Bar Graph from Excel Using data from SAS Visual Analytics

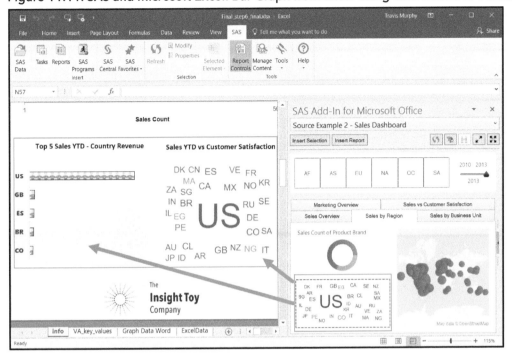

A few final touches for this element include the custom title and some bold text on the axis, which provide the last edits for this step in the example.

Step 3: Add the Key Values from SAS Visual Analytics

Now you repeat the steps above to insert the Key Value objects from your SAS Visual Analytics report. Do this on a new worksheet because we will be deriving the data to again use a native Excel element.

As seen in the following figure, you insert each key value into Excel and then use the SAS ribbon option to extract graph data, as you did in the previous step. The following are the metrics you are adding to your design:

1. Order Total (SUM $)
2. Sales Rep % of Target (Average %)
3. Vendor Satisfaction (Average %)

This means that we edit the function with a simple click and select the SAS Key Value data from the previous step. Do this for each of the items in your infographic and follow the numbers 1, 2, and 3 to assign the correct data.

Figure 11.12. SAS and Microsoft Excel: SAS Key Value Objects, Extracted Graph Fata for Use in the Infographic with Microsoft Excel Standard Functions

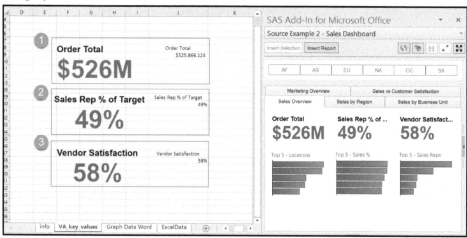

You now have data to use elsewhere in your infographic.

Return to your infographic worksheet to assign the data to the text elements as seen in Figure 11.13:

Figure 11.13. SAS and Microsoft Excel: Extracted Graph Data from SAS Key Value Objects Used in the Infographic with Microsoft Excel Functions

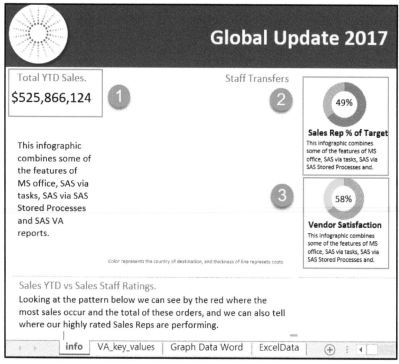

This means that we edit the function with a simple click and select the SAS Key Value data from the previous step. Do this for each of the items in your infographic and follow the numbers 1, 2, and 3 to assign the correct data.

NOTE: Using SAS Tasks in Microsoft Office

We do not use the options in the **Tasks** panel in SAS Add-In for Microsoft Office in these examples. However. they are very powerful self-service analytics for the business analyst to leverage. They include many powerful functions, and the wizards also extend to match the analytic packages you have installed on the SAS server. This means that a user can do high-end analytical functions, such as those in SAS Enterprise Guide, without leaving Microsoft Office. Remember that all the calculations are done on the SAS server, which means you are not limited to computation on your own computer.

Step 4: Using a SAS Stored Process inside Microsoft Excel

Instead of using a task wizard, we will be leveraging a SAS stored process from the SAS server. This is a great option for the data science team to create reusable analytic modules, which could be a data process that includes a data visualization output.

Using the **Reports** option on the SAS ribbon, we will select the SAS stored process to use in this infographic. Navigate to the required SAS stored process using the **Reports** option on the SAS Ribbon.

Navigate to **Reports**, as we have done multiple times using the SAS Visual Analytics reports. However, we can also use any stored process. These stored processes can be secured, interactive via prompts, and extremely complex analytic processes. SAS stored processes can also be a customized and governed corporate analytic output like you can see in Figure 11.14.

Figure 11.14. SAS and Microsoft Excel: Inserting a SAS Stored Process into the Infographic for Customized Analytical Processes

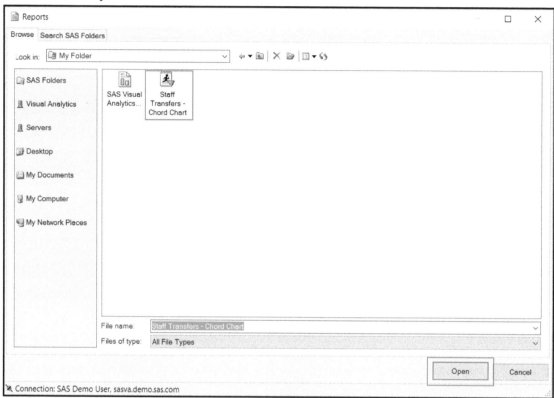

Navigate to the SAS stored process location and select **Stored Process ▶ Staff Transfers ▶ Global**. The example SAS file is provided in the files for this book, and you need to create a stored process from this code to use with this step in the example.

In this example, we use a SAS stored process that displays in a circle link graph the number and cost of internal company transfers of sales staff at our fictitious toy company. This allows us to leverage the great work done by the analytics team to generate this data and process. The code used inside this stored process was originally published in the SAS blog, and is a great example of SAS code that is a flexible data visualization and that leverages SAS ODS Graphics (Matange, 2016).

For more information about creating and managing a SAS stored process, please see SAS Institute (2014) in the bibliography.

Step 5: Tell SAS Where to Put the SAS Stored Process Output

Once you click open, as seen in the previous figure, you are then prompted to select the worksheet cell where you want the element inserted.

Figure 11.15. SAS Stored Process: Using the SAS Stored Process Enables Reuse of Custom Analytic Processes

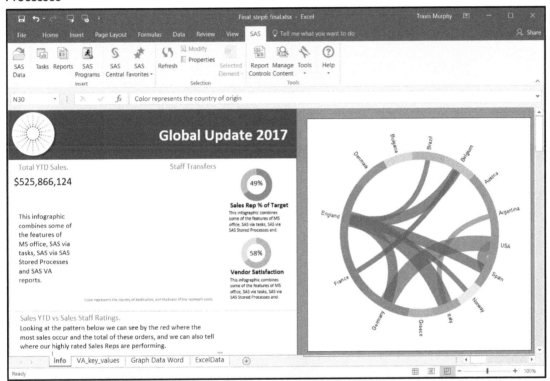

You might consider inserting the element in a cell that is not on your final design for the main infographic first and then moving the element into final position toward the end of your design process. This helps keep the infographic canvas free for other use within the worksheet cells, as shown in Figure 11.16:

Figure 11.16. SAS Stored Process: Moving the SAS Stored Process Output into Your Infographic

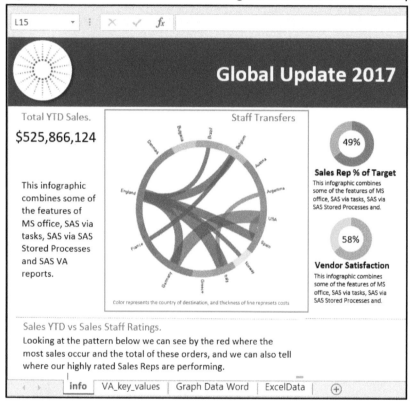

Step 6: Move the SAS Stored Process Output to the Desired Location in the Infographic

In Figure 11.16, the SAS stored process output is moved to the main area of the infographic in the top middle section, in between our other data-driven elements. Now the infographic has some SAS stored process elements, mixed with some Microsoft Excel charts and some SAS Visual Analytics report elements.

This example truly mixes the power of SAS and the features of Microsoft Excel, and extends the capabilities for the business analyst.

Using SAS Code Directly inside Microsoft Excel

Using the SAS code feature inside the SAS Add-In for Microsoft Office, secured by administrators, you can submit code directly from Microsoft Office (see Figure 11.17). This is a very powerful feature that has been added over the recent releases of SAS Add-In for Microsoft Office. This feature can provide data and graphics to the Excel spreadsheet and can still be secure and governed from the corporate platform. This is a great option if you have the skills and requirement to execute SAS code, and is excellent if you have regular custom scripts that you use for your analysis.

Figure 11.17. Example SAS Programs Dialog: A power user can leverage SAS from directly inside Microsoft Excel with SAS Add in for Microsoft Office

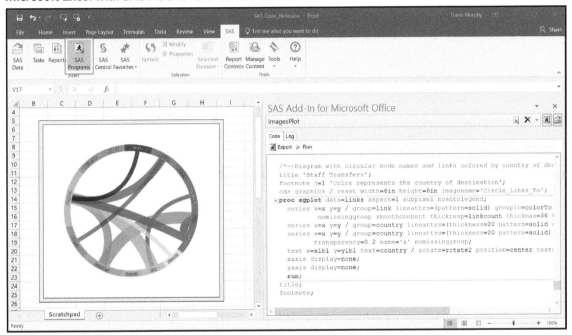

Now, even though you don't have to use this in your example, as we have all the visual elements we need, we could run the code from the SAS stored process example directly from within this window, making you less reliant on IT teams and data science teams in your organization.

Step 7: The Final Touches

Like the previous example, now that the data is in the infographic, some formatting and updates to the text headings and comments might be required. These subjective steps will add the final touches and make the infographic tell your story. Microsoft Excel does not format your design as easily as Microsoft PowerPoint because each productivity tool is very different from the other. Excel has enabled us to use a variety of data and visual options that are specific to capabilities of the tool. Once again, use this step to confirm that the context is clear for the intended audience of the infographic and that you have enough text and commentary. Here are a few examples of final touches:

- **Text and images** – Add subjective context and custom images between the visuals and the story.

- **Placement** – Alignment, spacing, and scale are key to getting the infographic just right.

- **Colors** – SAS objects are being displayed as the SAS Visual Analytics report was set. These can be changed in SAS and automatically refreshed in Excel. Other colors for background and text within Excel are worth revisiting here.

Step 8: Share the Infographic

When you are happy with the final touches, you should save the output. Instead of selecting the standard document type (XLSX format), you can choose either the HTML format or PDF format to save the entire infographic that is ready for sharing. Figure 11.18 shows the final infographic.

Figure 11.18. Final XLS Infographic: SAS and Microsoft Excel Used to Create this Data-Driven Infographic

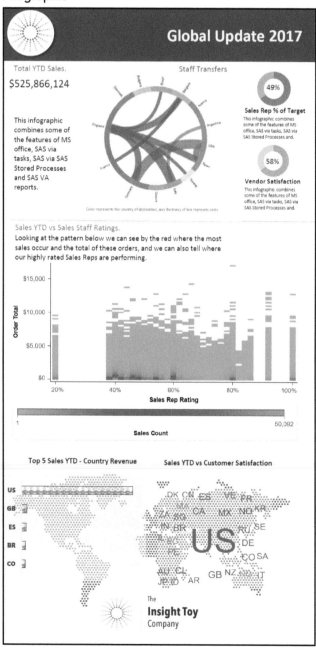

If you do want others to edit your design, you can just email the document to reviewers for their review and editing. They can update the data only if they have security permissions for the SAS analytics platform.

In Example 1, I highlighted the reason to use Microsoft Office combined with SAS. I believe that SAS and Microsoft Office combined assist with repeatability, scalability, and approachability for more users. This could prove to be a very popular combination in your organization for getting your data to your users.

Examples Gallery

Figures 11.19 and 11.20 are some additional examples of SAS and Microsoft Excel for creating infographics.

Figure 11.19. Example 1: SAS and Microsoft Excel: Data from SAS Visual Analytics and Some Native Microsoft Excel Graphs

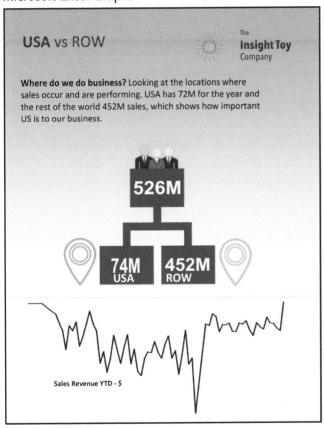

Figure 11.20. Example 2: SAS and Microsoft Excel – All data elements from SAS VA formatted in Microsoft Excel

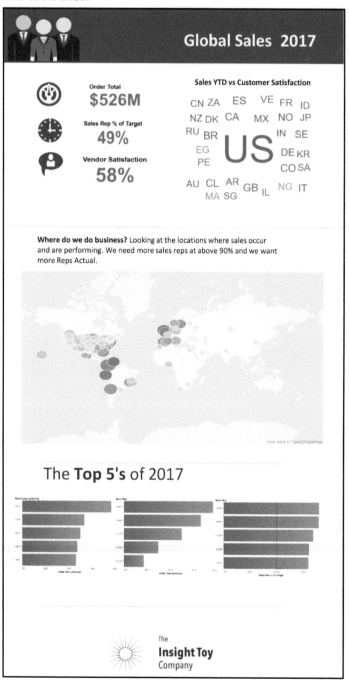

Chapter 12

Example 3: SAS Visual Analytics Infographic Inspired Dashboards

Overview

The primary focus of SAS Visual Analytics is to analyze and visualize any data. It makes sense to show that it can also be used in this context to create reports with infographics. In Example 1 and Example 2, we already used existing reports from SAS Visual Analytics as the source for other infographics. Example 3 shows how to create these SAS Visual Analytics reports and dashboards, and how to enhance them with infographic concepts.

Audience

This chapter is for SAS Visual Analytics users. Other users can gain an appreciation for SAS Visual Analytics and use the ideas presented here in order to articulate their own requirements.

Sample Files

Completed SAS Visual Analytics report examples are provided for reference along with the data and image files that are needed to reproduce these examples.

All files are provided for download here:

http://support.sas.com/murphy

Step 1: Start with Your Idea and Rough Design

Example 3 might be considered to be the best of both worlds: traditional dashboards and infographics.

Remember, if you want to save time in any infographics creation process, you should start with a whiteboard or piece of paper and get it all out of your head and into the world. This step should provide ideas for topic, context, questions I want to answer or highlight, and design ideas.

Figure 12.1 shows an initial mock-up.

Figure 12.1. Initial Mock-Up and Design of an Infographic with SAS Visual Analytics

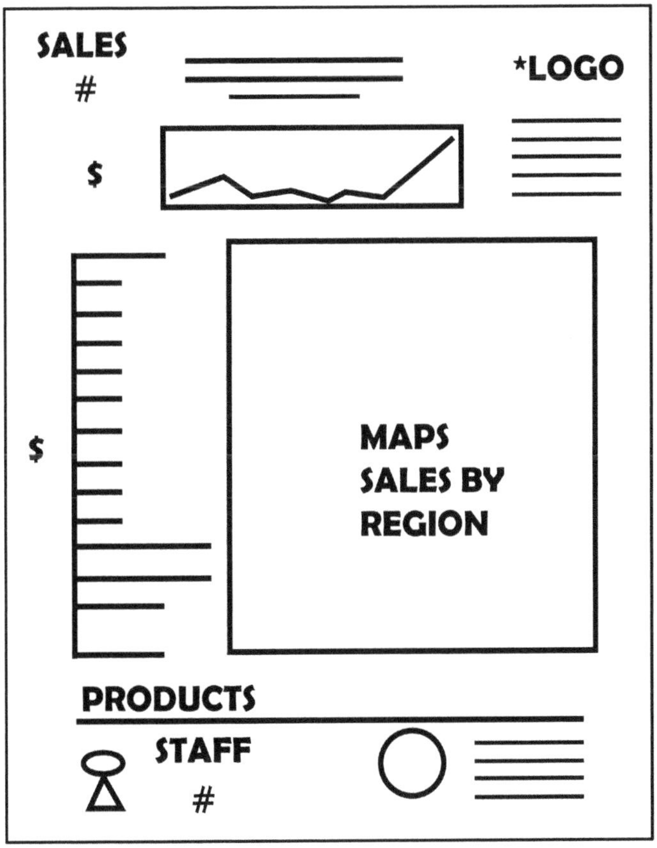

As you see, the ideas of the story are taking shape without using software. This step helps with ideas and the initial vetting of what matters and what does not matter to the story that we are trying to tell in the infographic. This can also highlight scale and white space in the design, which is good to understand before you start to drag elements onto the canvas.

Step 2: Explore Your Data

Familiarizing yourself with the data at the beginning of the project is essential. Consider these tips to further understand your data:

- Refer to your data dictionary (Appendix A) for an understanding of the data.
- Use the data load screen in SAS Visual Analytics which provides a data profile tab before you even load the data to understand the data contents before you start analyzing.
- Use the **Measure Details** option in SAS Visual Analytics to quickly understand the summary information.
- Explore the data using SAS Visual Analytics drag-and-drop options.

Now you have some data. Here are your choices:

- Jump right into the data.
- Create a new report.
- Open an existing report.

Figure 12.2 shows the choices:

Figure 12.2. Welcome Screen SAS Visual Analytics Choices

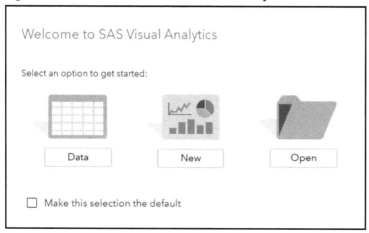

The quickest option is **Data**. The following figure shows the selection of VA_SAMPLE_SMALLINSIGHT, which has already been loaded into SAS Visual Analytics (see Figure 12.3).

Figure 12.3. SAS Visual Analytics Open Data Source Window

If you were working on your own data, you could load the data from the **Import** tab in this view, or you would ask your administrator for help to identify the data source that is available in your SAS Visual Analytics system. Figure 12.4 identifies these data options.

Figure 12.4. Data Options in SAS Visual Analytics

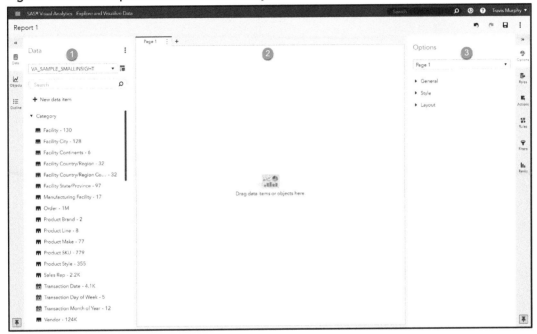

Each circled number corresponds to the part of the window that contains these specific features:

- ❶ Contains three panels, one each for Data, Objects, and Outline.
- ❷ Provides a canvas (destination for drag-and-drop operations) for designing your report.
- ❸ Gives access to other context-sensitive menus such as properties, filters and ranks, actions for interactivity, and roles for data allocation for each object.

The **Objects** panel is where all elements of our report will be dragged from and inserted onto the report canvas.

You can start by creating a fresh report and add some objects (such as bar graphs, line graphs and cross tabs) to get a clearer understanding of the profile and shape of your data. It is up to you to decide what to include at this stage. We are not creating the infographic at this point. We are in exploration phase and are developing a preliminary analysis of how the data could be used to build the infographic. Figure 12.5 shows a typical exploration.

Figure 12.5. Using SAS Visual Analytics to Explore the Data

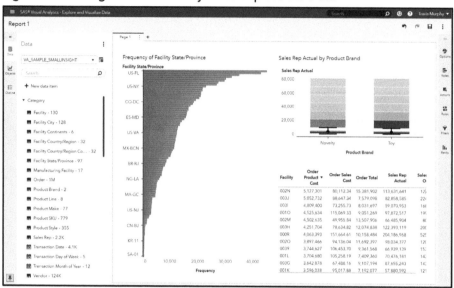

Step 3: Build the Basic Infographic

You can either create a new report, which will provide you with a blank canvas, or open an existing report to use as a template.

As shown in Figure 12.2, after you log on to SAS Visual Analytics, you can choose an appropriate option for creating your infographic. The quickest option is **Data**.

In this example, the data is already loaded in SAS Visual Analytics, and the table is called VA_SAMPLE_SMALLINSIGHT. If you don't have the data loaded yet, then use the **Import** tab to load the data into SAS Visual Analytics.

To start, let's create a strawman design and use the container object. Figure 12.6 shows how the container objects are used to provide the overall structure to the infographic design. Examples of container properties are background color and height. We are going to add three containers to our canvas in order to impose structure to our design. We can simply drag and drop these onto the canvas. We can assign these names and properties to the containers:

①   Top Container – Set the background to blue and the height to 20.
②   Middle Container – Set the height to 70.
③   Bottom Container – Set the background to blue and the height to 10.

Figure 12.6. SAS Visual Analytics Container Objects.

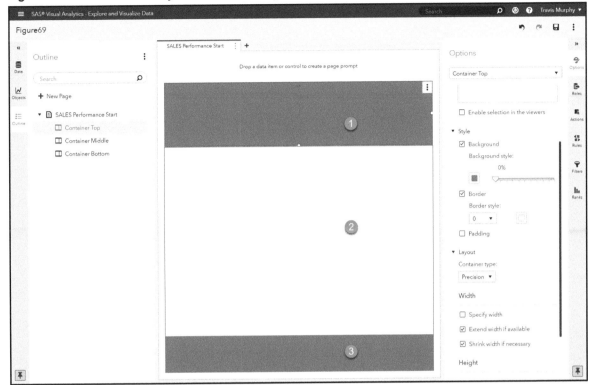

NOTE: Report Containers

The container is an object that controls the behavior of any other objects that are added to them. A container in SAS Visual Analytics can be set to have the following properties:

Standard – enables the objects to fit in the available space.

Precision – enables full control over where the content is placed.

Stack – enables the content to be stacked so that you can have more than one element in the same allocated space.

You can nest containers within containers to provide more control over design elements in your SAS Visual Analytics infographic inspired dashboard. For example, to control a group of objects as if they were a single object, you could use a container to bind them together. You could also set properties such as width and height for the container one time only, which would eliminate the need to set the properties for each of the other objects within the container.

Note that a container is not always required. The layout and the objects in a report determine whether you use the simple drag-and-drop method (with intelligent drop zones) or a container. I find that containers are a great way to organize the objects in SAS Visual Analytics. However, containers are not required to start designing your report or dashboard. You can just drag objects to the desired location if that works for your design.

You can see in Figure 12.7 that the container object provides a rough wireframe design for the infographic.

Figure 12.7. SAS Visual Analytics Outline Panel

> **NOTE: Naming Objects in a Report**
>
> As a best practice and a method to improve ease of use with your SAS Visual Analytics design, it is best to name the objects using the **Options** panel or to directly edit the names in the **Outline** panel. If you do this from the beginning, then you, and anyone else who uses the report, will have a much clearer idea of the elements in the report. You can use the **Outline** view to select each specific object in order to edit properties and context-sensitive options.

Now that you have the general layout using containers, we can add the remaining objects that we need for the rest of the infographic-inspired dashboard. Add the following objects to your design. You can add the data as you go or after you have all the objects on the canvas. Don't worry if you drag the object onto the wrong location. You can change the location of the object at any time using the **Outline** panel, the click-and-drag method on the canvas, or the **Undo** button.

Objects are the elements that you want in your infographic, and there are many to choose from. Not all are designed for data, but most of the objects are for data inside SAS Visual Analytics. You add these objects by drag-and-drop using the **Objects** panel on the left as shown in Figure 12.8.

Figure 12.8. Objects Panel in SAS Visual Analytics

You can add static text and data-driven text from the **Objects** panel. The inclusion of data is a great way to literally tell a story with the numbers. Your narrative can come to life with some facts to highlight in-line with the text. Icons and images are powerful non-data elements to add to the context within the infographic. Data-driven figures, or key values, with headlines are a great way to call out some important numbers for your infographic.

From the **Objects** panel, you can add the following objects to the **Top Container** of the infographic.

To frame our story, let's add some time context to the infographic. You can do this by adding a filter to the infographic to enable you to show one year at a time. The time element instantly makes this infographic more useful and reusable. Add the drop-down list object to the page level prompts at the top of your infographic. Assign the **Transaction Date – Year** data item to the drop-down list using the roles panel. This user defined filter provides context for every object that we include from here on.

Sales Performance: Set Up Our Basic Infographic

Figure 12.9 shows the objects inside **Top Container**:

Figure 12.9. Top Container Objects

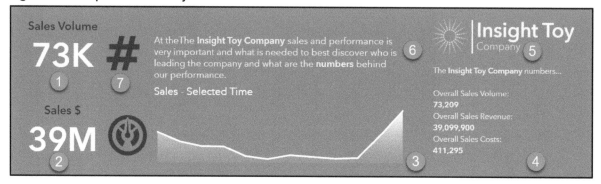

Top Container

Data Objects

❶ Show the count of orders placed for the selected year. You must add a Key Value object for sales volume. Use the **Options** panel to title it **Sales Volume**. Also, use this panel to specify the size and position settings for the desired location on the canvas. You then use the **Roles** panel to assign sales count to the measures role, which will create a single aggregated value in our infographic. Note that the text color and settings can be leveraged quickly by duplicating the object for use elsewhere in the infographic. This is especially useful for inheriting settings and properties after you have spent some time to get things just right on one object. Then, you just update the data on the **Roles** panel and you are done.

❷ Show the total revenue for orders placed in the selected year. To determine the total revenue, you must add a Key Value object for Sales Revenue ($). Use the **Options** panel to title it **Sales $**. You then use the **Roles** panel to assign Order Total to the measures role, which will create a single aggregated value in our infographic.

❸ Show the total $ of orders placed for the selected year over time. You must add a Line Chart for Sales $ Over Selected Time. Use the **Options** panel to title it **Sales $**. Also, use this panel to specify the size and position settings for the desired location on the canvas. You then use the **Roles** panel to assign, Order Total and Transaction Day – MMMYYY, which will create a single line chart in our infographic.

❹ Show key summary numbers and some additional text commentary for the selected year. You must add a text object with dynamic text. Use the **Options** panel to title it **Key Numbers**. Also, use this panel to specify the size and position settings for the desired location on the canvas. You then use the **Roles** panel to assign Order Total, Frequency, and Order Sales Cost, which will enable them to be used inline within your text object. You can tell a story with numbers and free text in the single object.

Remember that the entire infographic returns data in the context of the selected year. This is due to the drop-down list (page filter) that we added earlier in the example.

Non-data Elements

⑤ Add the image object, which is the company logo for the Insight Toy Company.

⑥ Add a text object for an overview and purpose of the infographic. This provides a description for the audience to gain some context.

⑦ Add another image to provide a visual reference for the key value number and KPI/Gauge in the infographic. These are muted colors to ensure that the data is the focus

Middle Container

Figure 12.10 shows the objects in the **Middle Container**:

Figure 12.10. Middle Container Objects

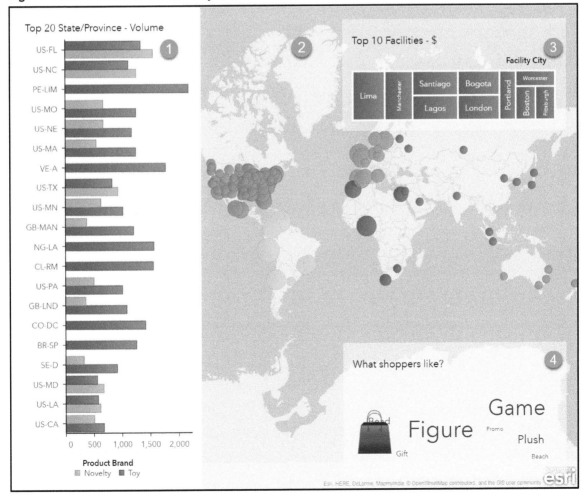

Data-Driven Objects

① Show the total count of orders that are placed for the Top 20 states and provinces. Add a bar graph for Sales $ Over Selected Time. Use the **Options** panel to title it **Top 20 State/Province – Sales Volume**. Also, use this panel to specify the size and position settings for the desired location on the canvas. You then use the **Roles** panel to assign State/Province and Frequency, and add a group role of Product Brand, which will create a bar graph in our infographic. Use the **Rank** panel and apply a Top 20 ranking.

② Show the total revenue by city on a map. Add a Geo Map object. Use the **Options** panel to title it **Company Map**. Also, use this panel to specify the size and position settings for the desired location on the canvas. You then use the **Roles** panel to assign Facility City and Order Total. Then, add a color role of Region to color the map in groups of cities. Use the **Options** panel again to change the map provider setting, select ESRI, and change the map to the World Light Grey Base to fit with the desired theme for this infographic.

③ Show the Top 10 facilities for sales in the specified period using a Treemap object. Use the **Options** panel to title it **Top 10 Facilities $**. Also, use this panel to specify the size and position settings for the desired location on the canvas. You then use the **Roles** panel to assign Facility City and Order Total. You can overlay the Geo Map with this.

④ Show the Top selling products in the specified period using a Word Cloud object. Use the **Options** panel to title it **Word Cloud Product Line $**. Also, use this panel to specify the size and position settings for the desired location on the canvas. You then use the **Roles** panel to assign Product Line and Order Total. You can overlay the Geo Map with this.

Non-data Objects

Add an image object to show the shoppers bag icon next to the product line word cloud.

Bottom Container

Figure 12.11 shows the objects in **Bottom Container**:

Figure 12.11. Bottom Container Objects

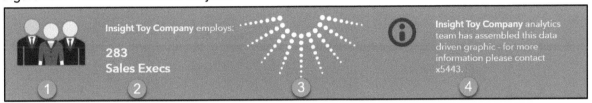

Data Objects

❷ Show the total number of Sales Executives our company employs. By adding a text object that contains dynamic text. Use the **Options** panel to title it **Sales Execs**. Also, use this panel to specify the size and position settings for the desired location on the canvas. You then use the **Roles** panel to assign data, Sales Person (count). Then, you can use static and dynamic text in your text object.

Non-data Objects

❶ Add another image to provide a visual reference for the staff numbers in the infographic. These are muted colors to ensure that the data is the focus.

❸ Add the image object, which is the company logo for the Insight Toy Company.

❹ Add text for contact information for the audience.

As you can see in Figure 12.12, the infographic is taking shape. It might be ready, as is, to tell our story. However, for the purpose of this exercise, we can enhance the infographic with some additional content to illustrate what is possible.

Figure 12.12. Finished Infographic

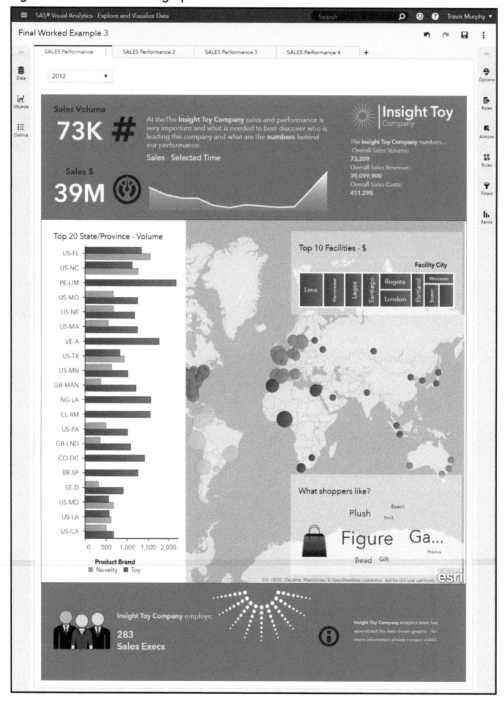

Step 4: Add some Approachable Analytics

Geo Maps: Bringing Data to Life

You already have included some approachable analytics in your existing design because of the default geographic analysis features in SAS. I like to use geo maps to personalize the infographic with interactive drive-time analysis and other options. The geo map feature is enabled by default in the preceding figure. You can use the search icon in the corner of the map to try it yourself.

Used in the previous step, ESRI options are included in SAS, and the map that you selected is from the available maps on the public ESRI server.

Add Some Advanced Analytics

This option is provided to show you that it is easy to introduce approachable analytics into your data visualization projects.

There are many options for leveraging more advanced analytics-driven visualizations inside your infographics. Here are a few options for business users to consider:

Cluster Analysis

Using clusters is a great way to tell a story from the data that is based on analytic models. I like the parallel coordinates plot because it shows colorful patterns for static views of the data. It is also effective when used interactively because it can clearly highlight common groups within the data.

Network Analysis

Using a network is a great way to show relationships within the data. A good example is the products that are part of each product line. This can be powerful when you enable a map as a background to the network. All you need is to use a geographic data item to unlock the network view on a map.

Sankey Diagrams

Using a Sankey diagram is excellent for both static and interactive viewers. You can see common paths that are taken by customers in many contexts. This is great to visualize the customer's journey through many contexts such as their use of your marketing channels or the events that lead to customer churn.

Add Analytics Objects to Examples

Add the following objects to the infographic. Two objects need to be from the **Objects** panel to your infographic. First, insert a parallel coordinates plot to the bottom container, which is already set as a precision container, and now you can add your data roles to this object. Then, add a network diagram, which is composed of nodes (values) and links (relationships). Our goal is to show Sales $ and Product Hierarchy in two levels of this hierarchy.

You can apply additional analytics to the containers for the infographic in this example.

Top Container

No changes are necessary for **Top Container**.

Middle Container

Data-Driven Objects

The following are changes to make to existing objects in the infographic. We create additional space in the **Middle Container** to accommodate the migration of objects from **Bottom Container**.

- Resize the bar graph object to create space for the other objects being migrated to this container.
- Move the text object from Bottom Container to Middle Container.
- Move the Word Cloud object under the bar graph object.
- There are no changes to the Geo Map object.
- Move the Treemap object lower in the container, maintain overlay on the Geo Map object.

Non-data Objects

Move the images, the shopping bag, and the staff icon to align with other objects in this container.

Bottom Container

Most changes occur in **Bottom Container**.

Data Objects

Show the sales for the product brands and the product lines within each brand. Add a network object to show these sales. Use the **Options** panel to title it "**Product Network**". Also, use this panel to select the size and position settings for the desired location on the canvas. Also, you want to ensure that it is a hierarchical network. You then use the **Roles** panel to assign Product Hierarchy, and the **Size** role as the order total. To show more of the data in the one visual, change the number of levels to 2. See Figure 12.13 for a view of **Bottom Container**:

Figure 12.13. Network Visualization and a Parallel Coordinates Plot Added to the Infographic

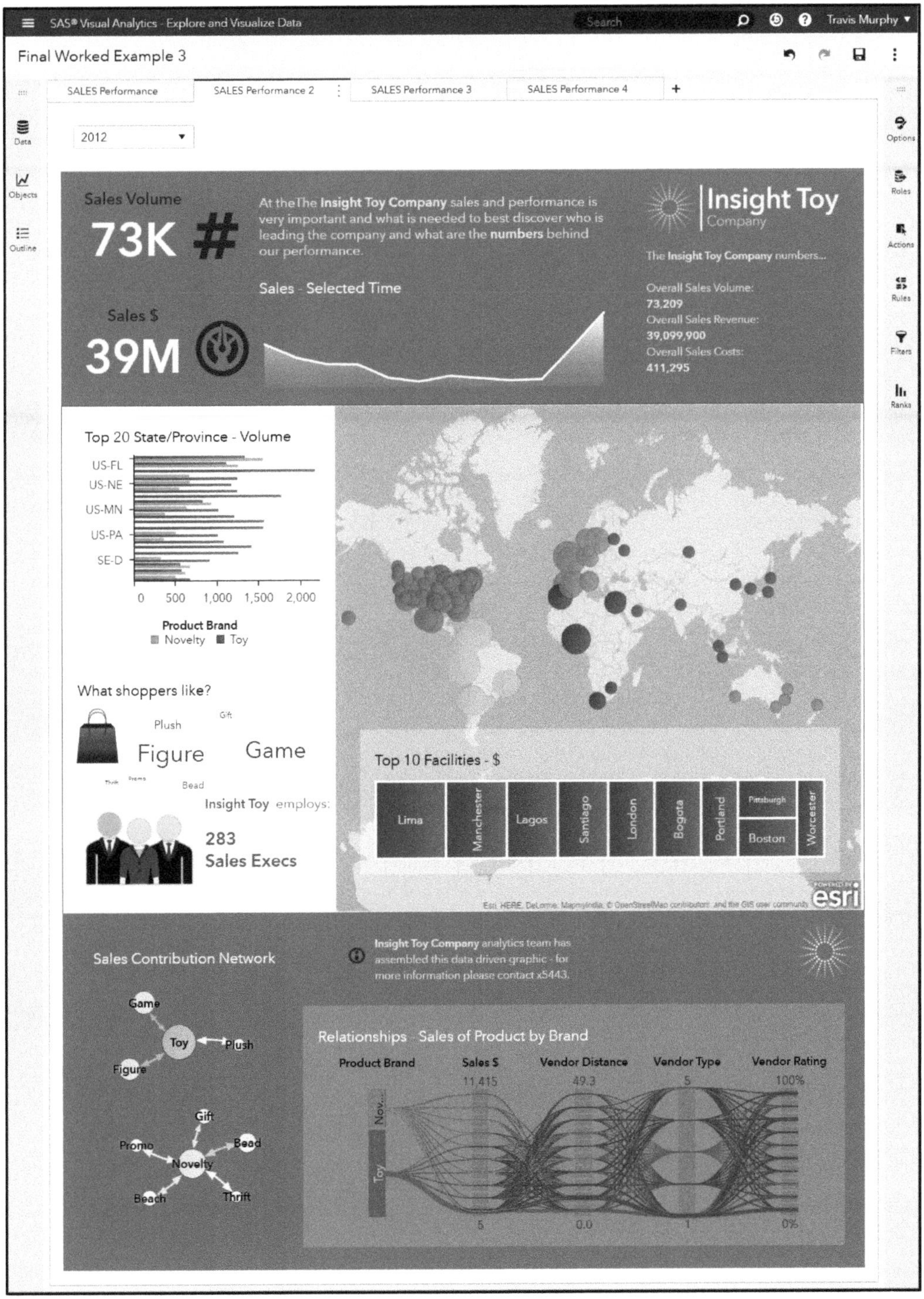

Next, show the common factors for sales by product line. Add a parallel coordinates plot object. Use the **Options** panel to title it **Relationships – Sales of Product by Brand**. Also, use this panel to specify the size and position settings for the desired location on the canvas. You then use the **Roles** panel to assign Product Line, Sales $, Vendor Distance, Vendor Type, and Vendor Rating. This will cluster the common elements together and show bands for each product line. See the preceding figure for a view of **Bottom Container**.

Non-data Objects

The non-data objects in Bottom Container have a few minor changes. Replace the white flare logo with a white full flare logo. Also, resize and position it in the right corner of the container. Move information text and image objects to their new positions within the container as shown in the preceding figure.

Step 5: Add External Graphics

Add Custom Data-Driven Content

Adding a third-party chart object to your infographic can be a powerful visual enhancement.

This step is advanced, but not because data-driven content is used in the infographic, but rather how the data-driven content is *created* to use in the infographic. The creation of this reusable content requires skills in coding for the web and understanding what SAS will pass to the content. Check the SAS communities to learn more about creating data-driven content objects.

NOTE: Data-Driven Content Object

Data-Driven Content is an object type that enables users to create their own custom visualization while still using the SAS Visual Analytics user interface and query engine for assigning data, applying filters and ranks, and so on. This object is similar to the Web Content object where a URL must be provided in order for the custom content to be displayed in your report. However, the Data-Driven Content object requires data, specifically data from SAS. When data is not assigned, the object displays a warning until data has been assigned.

The Data-Driven Content object is located in the **Other** group of the **Objects** panel.

Data-Driven Content can be the source or target of interactions (or both the source and the target), but it must be coded into the custom content. The Data-Driven Content developer must use specific events to detect selections or broadcast selections or to detect and broadcast selections in order to achieve this interactivity.

Results of the SAS query for the assigned data roles will be provided to the custom content in a specific structure. The content author must have designed the object to consume and parse that data structure to render the custom visualizations in the desired format and display.

Data-Driven Content should also be designed to show sample data and some information using text and images to help inform and guide the SAS user in getting the most from the custom content.

In many cases, users will select the SAS component as visual objects that have been optimized for all devices and data scenarios. However, sometimes you might want a particular visualization that tells a particular story from your data. It could be a calendar chart, a spiral chart, or even a 3D map of Earth using Google Earth. SAS can include third-party objects within SAS Visual Analytics and give the user the best of both worlds. SAS will accept and extend the capabilities of these custom visual content and still leverage the benefits of the SAS platform. This feature unleashes the power of SAS into the world of data art and creativity.

Step 5a: Adding the Data-Driven Content: Example using the Condegram

This example uses a third-party graphic called the condegram spiral plot that was customized for use with this book and SAS Visual Analytics (Narechania, 2017). Figure 12.14 shows an example of a third-party visualization that has been edited to enable use with SAS Visual Analytics.

Figure 12.14. Condegram Spiral Plot: JavaScript Graphic (Image credit, A. Narechania, 2017)

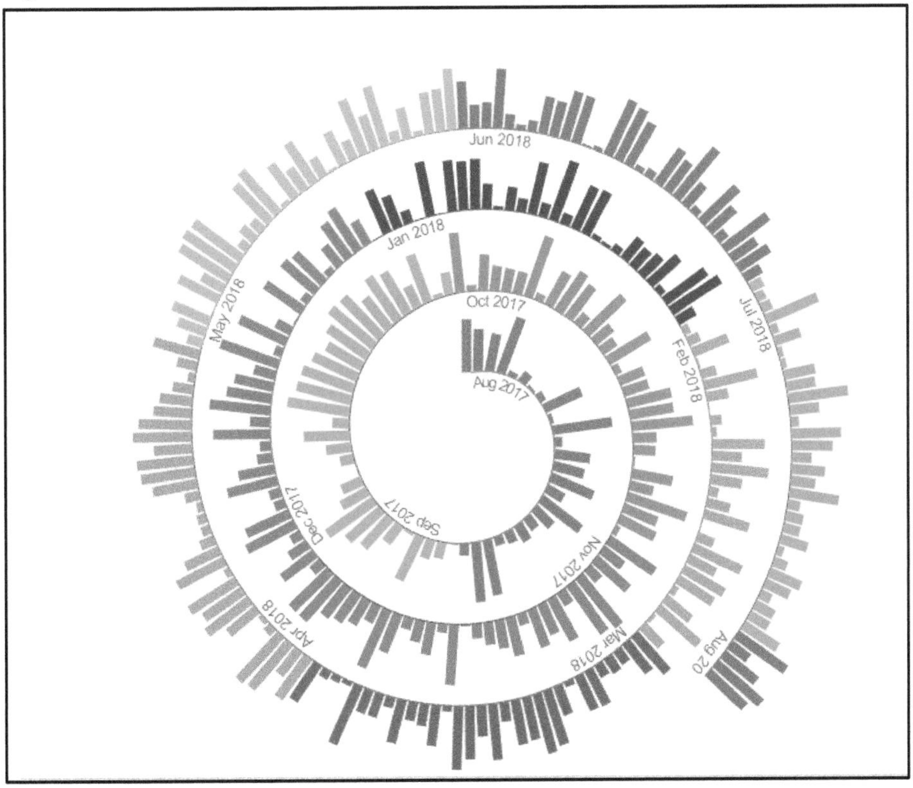

Using the data-driven content object in your infographic is the easy part. Go to the **Objects** panel and drag the data-driven content onto the canvas, and remove the line graph and the Treemap (tile chart) from the current design. The harder part is creating this object that is ready for use in SAS Visual Analytics. My colleague, Falko Schulz, who is a SAS developer, edited this open source graph in this example according to my requirements for this book. The sample HTML document is provided to show the additions for the data-driven content object.

Insert the Data-Driven Content object, the condegram timeline, and then assign the order amount by transaction day on the **Roles** panel. You can also interact with this object to filter your condegram for only the required data. Your data roles must be a date and a measure. If you want more roles and settings, then the person who designs your data- driven content object or custom visualization must set it up first.

Step 5b: Adding Data-Driven Content: Third-Party Graphic

To add a third-party graphic to this infographic example, we will adjust the following elements inside SAS Visual Analytics.

Top Container

No changes are necessary for **Top Container**.

Middle Container

Data-Driven Objects

We need to clean house in the middle container to make space for an additional object: the data-driven content object.

Remove the Bar Graph and the Sales Execs text objects. Then, move the word cloud to the former location of the bar graph. Leave the Geo Map object as it is for now.

Change the Treemap to a Boxplot Object by using the snowman icon in the top right corner of the treemap. Select the Box Plot object from the **available** options and move the boxplot to the bottom container by drag-and-drop.

You now create a new object from the **Object** panel, the data-driven content object, and place it in the middle container under the word cloud. Use the **Options** panel to link this object to the condegram example. Then, use the **Roles** panel to assign the data to the object, order total and Transaction date – ddmmyy. This object should now render with data.

Non-data Objects

Move the image, the shopping bag, to align into the new design. Remove the staff image entirely from the design.

Bottom Container

Data-Driven Objects

Remove the parallel coordinates plot object from the design and realign the boxplot, which was moved from the middle container.

Non-data Objects

No changes are necessary for the non-data objects.

Figure 12.15 shows the result of the addition of the third-party data-driven content along with the edits to the three containers.

Figure 12.15. SAS Visual Analytics Dashboard with Infographic Elements

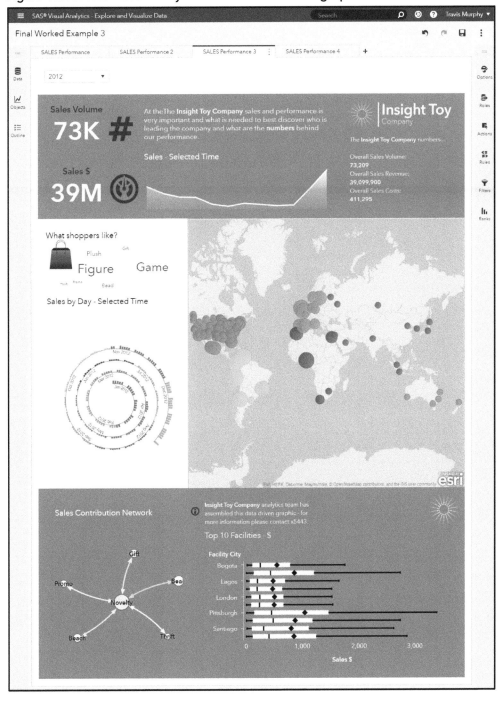

As seen in this example, SAS Visual Analytics can display more visuals than ever before, and allows users at all skill levels to develop their analytics skills, without restricting their storytelling options.

Step 6: Add Interactivity

Step 6a: Setting Automatic Actions

Even though, out of the box, SAS Visual Analytics is interactive, we can make this page interactive in many more ways by adding prompts for users to decide what to show, or by adding discrete actions to each element of the infographic using the **Actions** panel on the right. In this example, we can make this entire infographic interactive with a single mouse click. Select automatic actions on all objects as shown in Figure 12.16.

Figure 12.16. Actions Panel

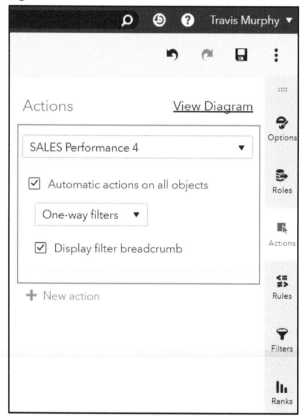

Step 6b: Adding an Additional Data-Driven Content Object

In this step, you will add an additional data-driven content object. However, this time, we will be using this object to show an image when specific data is selected. This data-driven content object will assess the product line name and show only the image that matches the selected product line name. Make the following changes to the infographic.

Top Container

No changes are necessary for **Top Container.**

Middle Container

Data-Driven Objects

- Move the Geo Map object to the left side of the middle container.
- Move the Word Cloud object to the top left of the Geo Map object.
- Move the Data-Driven Content Object – link to Condegram. Place to the right side of the middle container.
- Add the New Object.
  - Data-Driven Content Object is a link to a dynamic image data-driven content object in product_image.html. Add the data role, product line from the available data items. When a product line is passed to this object, the object will fetch an image that matches this data to an image file from the web, and display the image in the container.

Non-data Objects

- Move the shoppers bag icon and align it with the new design.
- Add the new static image and point it to the color flare logo image for company branding. This object also fills in the blank space until data is passed to the dynamic product image, which is the data-driven content object.

Bottom Container

No changes are necessary for the **Bottom Container** in the infographic.

The following example (Figure 12.17) shows the result of the addition of interactivity along with the edits to the three containers.

Figure 12.17. SAS Visual Analytics Dashboard That Contains Infographics Displaying Interactivity

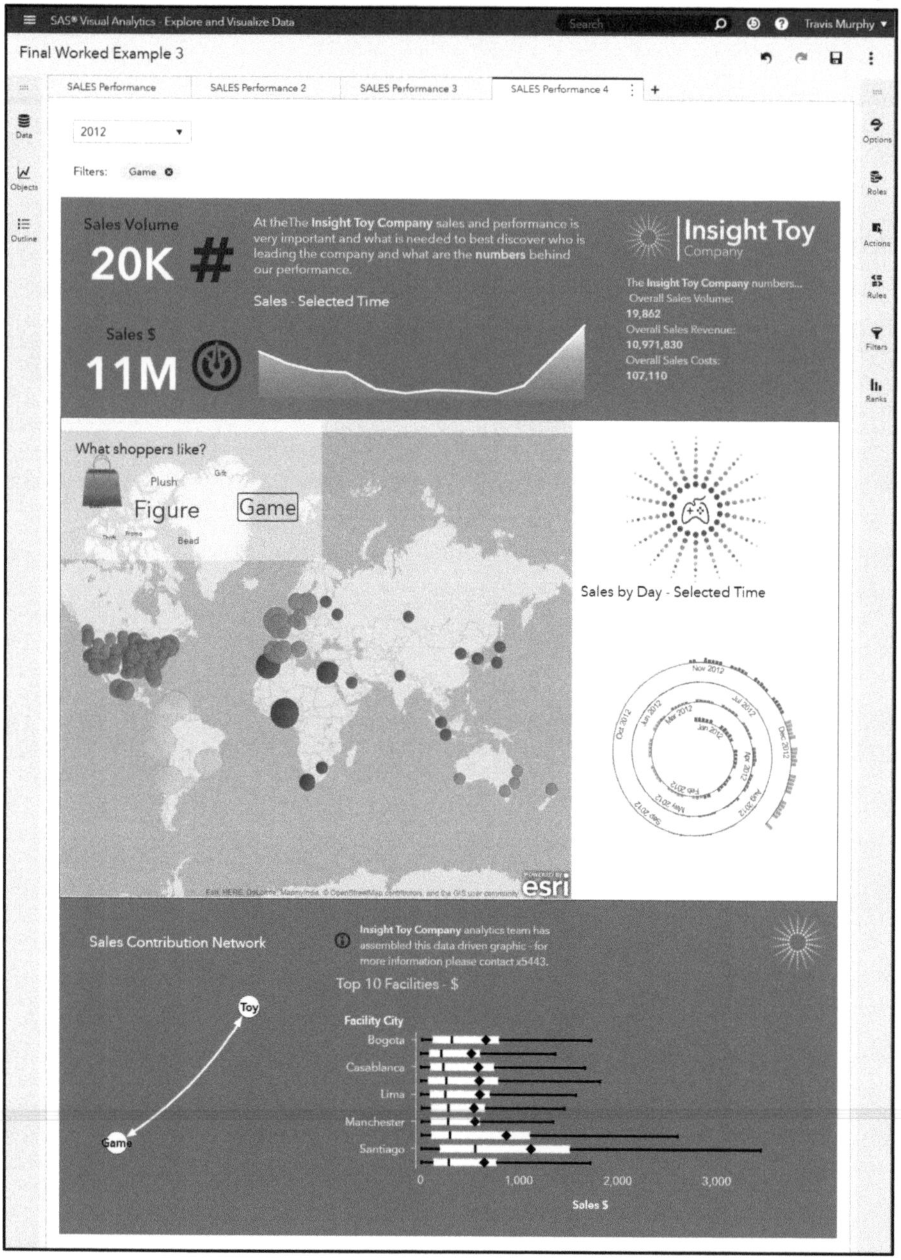

There are many ways to add interactivity into your infographic in SAS Visual Analytics. However, you have used the easiest method in only one setting. We already selected this setting in Step 6a, with the **Automatic Filters** option. Now, when you select the product line in the word cloud, you will show only the sales for that product line in your condegram (data-driven content object) and also a dynamic image for that product line in the preceding figure. For example, clicking the **Game** product line will show only Game sales, and also a picture of Game console above it.

There are many more controls to try in the **Actions** panel. You used the simplest and most dynamic option to link all actions to each other. The ribbon at the top of your infographic is updated with any filters that are applied in your interaction.

Step 7: Share the Infographic

You could now share the infographic by taking a screen capture of the image, or you could email the link to others so that they can provide access directly to SAS Visual Analytics. Sharing the infographic using SAS Visual Analytics provides options such as collaboration and commentary for the broader team who might want to assist in the design of the infographic.

SAS Visual Analytics can email directly from within the software to any user that is registered in the organization and also provide a secured link so that the data does not get in the wrong hands (see Figure 12.18).

Figure 12.18. Email from SAS Visual Analytics

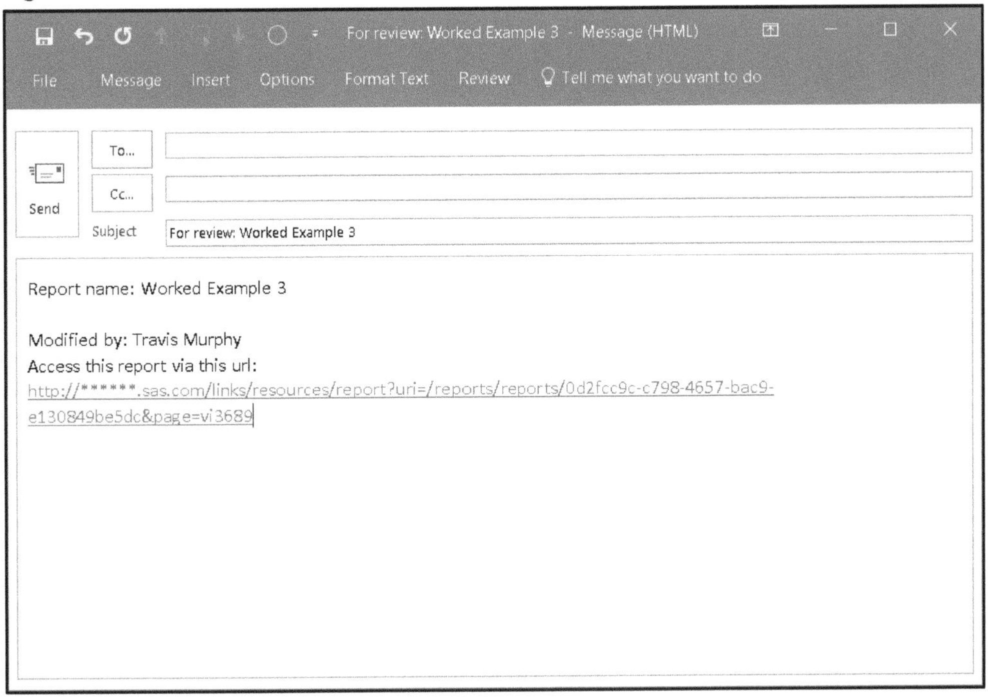

It is also worth noting that there are now APIs that allow you to call the elements of the SAS Visual Analytics dashboard and share it in whatever way you want. This now means you can create endless entry points into SAS Visual Analytics and display an entire dashboard or a single graph. This means that accessing your dashboard is easier than ever before and provides flexibility for how you display and share your data-driven visuals.

Examples Gallery

Figures 12.19–12.26 show additional examples of using SAS Visual Analytics to create dashboards that include infographics. Many examples in this section contain geographic elements in the designs, which are highly interactive and approachable for business users.

Figure 12.19. Example 1: College Basketball Infographic with SAS Visual Analytics (Image credit: F. Schulz, 2017)

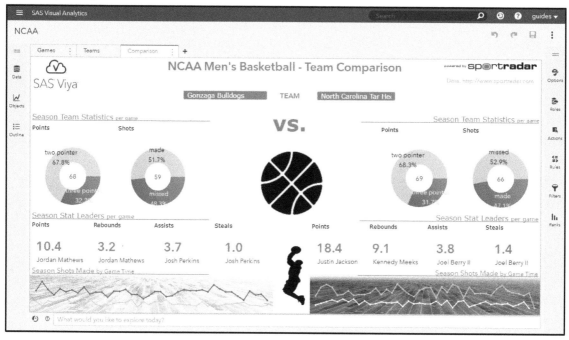

Figure 12.20. Example 2: Chicago Crime Infographic with SAS Visual Analytics (Image credit: F. Schulz, 2017)

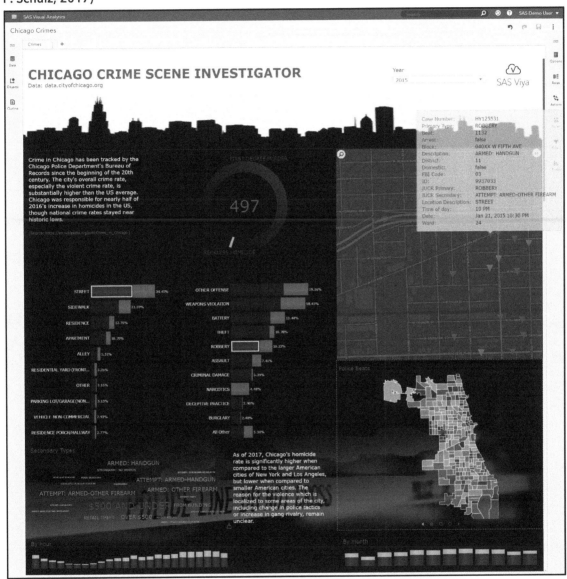

Figure 12.21. Example 3: Electricity Plant Capacity Infographic with SAS Visual Analytics (Image credit: F. Schulz, 2017)

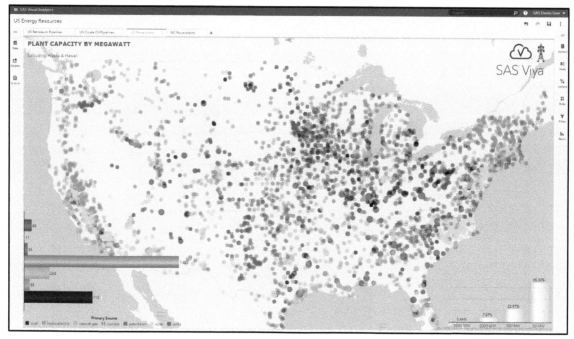

Figure 12.22. Example 4: Volcano Activity Infographic with SAS Visual Analytics (Image Credit: F. Schulz, 2017)

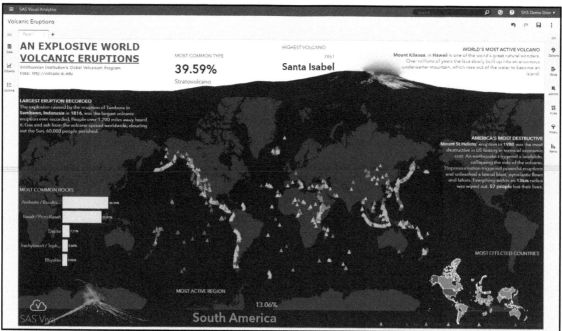

Figure 12.23. Example 5: Flights Cancelled Infographic with SAS Visual Analytics (Image credit: F. Schulz, 2017)

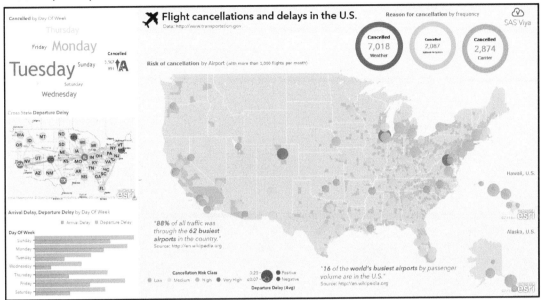

Figure 12.24. Example 6: Obesity Statistics by Age Infographic (Using Center for Disease Control Data) with SAS Visual Analytics (Image credit: F. Schulz, 2017)

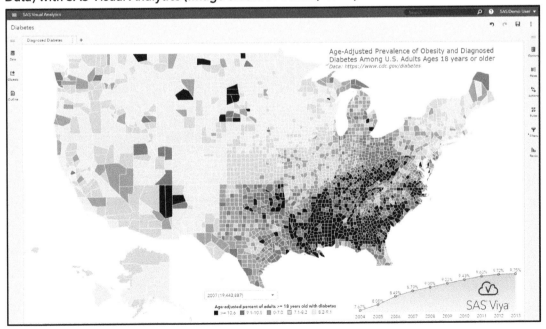

Figure 12.25. Example 7: World Pollution Infographic with SAS Visual Analytics (Image credit: F. Schulz, 2017)

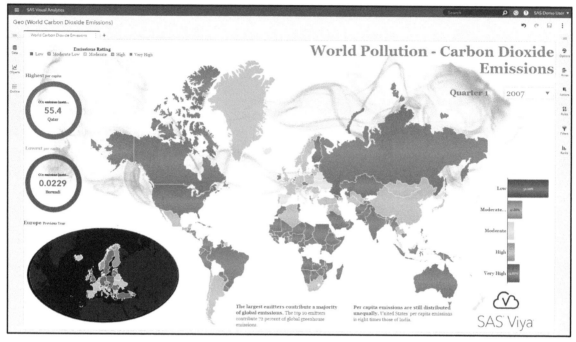

Figure 12.26. Example 8: Extraterrestrial Impacts Infographic with SAS Visual Analytics (Image credit: F. Schulz, 2017)

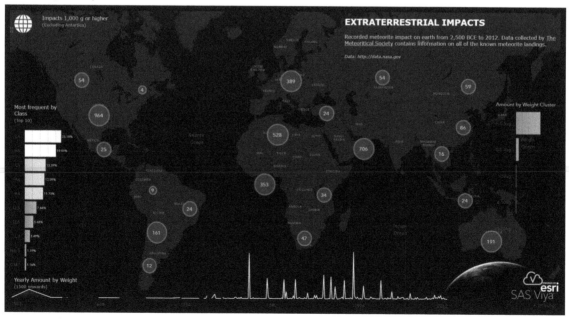

Chapter 13

Example 4: SAS Code to Create Infographics

Overview

Coding with SAS is a very powerful skill set for any data analyst, and this example will show the power of this approach. My SAS programming skills are not as advanced as the skills of some of my colleagues. However, this does not stop me from seeing the power and endless options that SAS code provides for anyone who is trying to visualize and analyze data. I enlisted help from my colleague, Dr. Robert Allison, a software development tester, to develop the code to support the SAS examples in this book. You might be familiar with Dr. Allison (or his moniker "The Graph Guy") via his blog called "SAS Graphics in Action!", his book, *SAS/GRAPH: Beyond the Basics* (Allison, 2012), and the worked examples that he has provided online for all

SAS users who want to get a jump start. I have used Dr. Allison's examples many times with SAS customers to show the options that they can use to leverage SAS in their organization. The following examples show how to use SAS code for data visualization for a business outcome: creating an infographic.

Audience

Although the examples in this chapter can be appreciated by all levels of users, to actually write this example requires advanced SAS programming skills. Therefore, Dr. Allison wrote the coded examples for me, based on my requirements for this book.

Sample Files

The required sample files contain the sample data and the SAS program (file type .sas). There are also a few required image files for the examples. All files are provided as part of the downloadable files for this book.

Using SAS Code for Data Visualization

This example creates an infographic with SAS Studio and SAS custom code. This example uses SAS/GRAPH to create a custom design. The code will show the power and flexibility of SAS with some of the complexities of the SAS platform in order to deliver a precise infographic.

The coding option is to do everything manually. For example, you build and design as a graphic artist, a data artist, or a data scientist. This option can create an analytics process to create everything automatically, from the data and the code. This means that you use SAS code, SAS/GRAPH and SAS Output Delivery System (ODS), to build the entire infographic. This is a precise and valid option to build infographics and leverage the power in the SAS analytics platform. However, you must be able to code in SAS. This is great for experienced SAS programmers, but is not an option for all users because SAS coding skills, like any programming skills, can take time to develop. However, you should jump in if you have interest in coding with SAS.

Example 4 is a custom design where you can achieve pixel-perfect results and create precise data- driven designs. Although the learning curve might be steep, it might be appropriate option when you need ultimate control and exact layout and formatting. In my experience, this option is excellent when working with a precise vision of the infographic that is required. Like any coding, it is often the work done before you start coding that makes the difference and saves a lot of time.

Example 4.1: Custom Business Infographic Poster

Step 1: Design

Remember, if you want to save time in any infographic creation process, you should start with a whiteboard or piece of paper and get it all out of your head and into the world. This step should provide ideas for topic, context, questions I want to answer or highlight, and design ideas. Figure 13.1 shows an initial mock-up.

Figure 13.1. Initial Mock-Up and Design of an Infographic

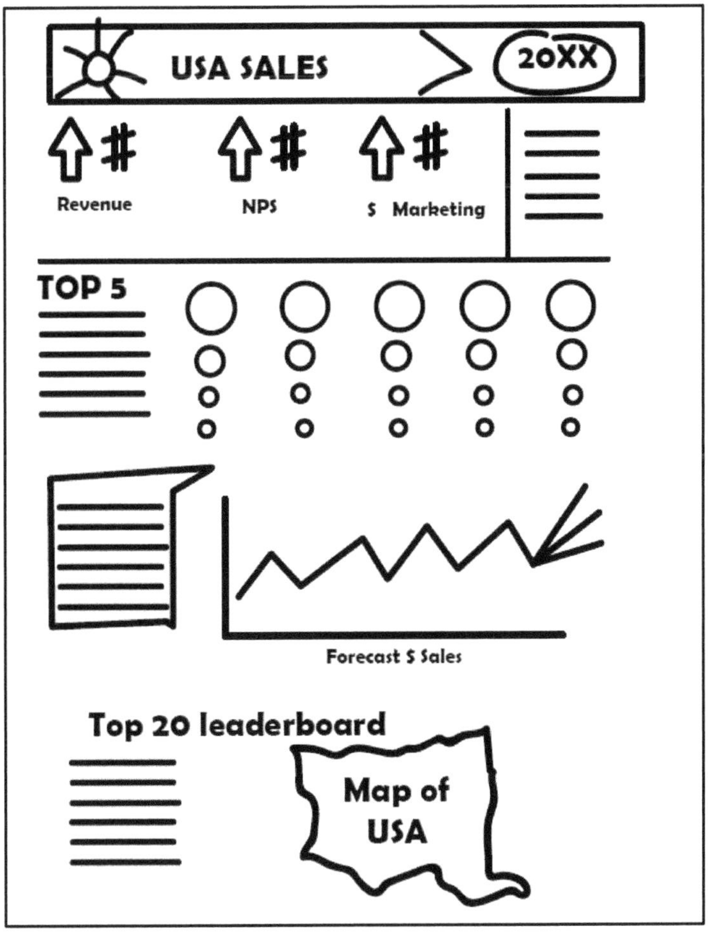

Step 2: Required Elements

What objects are needed from SAS and elsewhere? Let's break down the design to figure out the coding requirements.

Elements

Non-data Elements

- **Logo** – Use an image that is not driven by the data but is important for branding.
- **Text** – Use non-data-driven text elements that will provide the context for the data inside the infographic.
- **Palette** – Use the color scheme in the design that is an important element in the design and the corporate branding of the infographic.

Data Driven Elements

- **Top Five Products** – Use the data to rank the Top 5 products that we sell at the Insight Toy company.

- **Show dates in text** – Use the code to control the data that we use in the infographic. The code can be rerun in the future.

- **Box Plot** – Repeat a box plot for each city with outliers for sales that occur in each location.

- **Customer Satisfaction** – Show customer satisfaction for each city.

- **Map of USA sales locations** – Display a map that contains exploding text to show where these products are sold in the USA, satisfaction by color, and sales amount by size.

- **Forecast** – Show the sales of our two brands over a selected time period and a forecast of sales over the next 12 months.

- **Big Numbers** – Show single numbers and color-coded numbers based on the data.

Step 3: Walking through the Code

To avoid being overwhelmed, you don't have to review the approximately 1000 lines of code for the dashboard example in this book. Instead, it would be a good exercise to show a shortened version in the form of pseudocode to let you know in a high-level way how such an infographic is put together.

This section contains the code steps that are used to create the infographic. Each step that contains the pseudocode is following by an excerpt of SAS documentation that explains the SAS procedure that is used. First, let's create several graphs to be used on the dashboard. Here is the pseudocode for creating the graphs.

Note: For the full code, please refer to the sample files download for this book.

Program 13.1. Pseudocode for Creating Several Graphs

```
Proc gplot ...
Plot y*x / name='bubble';

Proc gplot ...
Plot y*x / name='lines';

Proc gplot ...
Plot y*x / name='box20';

Proc gmap ...
Choro / name='map20';
```

NOTE: PROC GPLOT

The SAS documentation introduces PROC GPLOT as follows:

The GPLOT procedure plots the values of two or more variables on a set of coordinate axes (X and Y). The coordinates of each point on the plot correspond to two variable values in an observation of the input data set. The procedure can also generate a separate plot for each value of a third (classification) variable. It can also generate bubble plots in which circles of varying proportions representing the values of a third variable are drawn at the data points.

The procedure produces a variety of two-dimensional graphs including the following plots:

- simple scatter plots
- overlay plots in which multiple sets of data points are displayed on one set of axes
- plots against a second vertical axis
- bubble plots
- logarithmic plots (controlled by the AXIS statement)

(For further details, see SAS/GRAPH(R) 9.3: Reference, Third Edition)

To place multiple SAS/GRAPH objects on a page, you can save them in grsegs, create a custom GREPLAY template (with spaces where you want each graph), and then replay the grsegs (graphs) into the GREPLAY template.

To save a graph in a GREPLAY template, use the NAME= option when you run PROC GRAPH.
Next, create a custom template using PROC GREPLAY where you lay out the areas to which these graphs are placed.

Program 13.2. SAS Code for Creating a Custom Template

```
proc greplay tc=tempcat nofs igout=work.gseg;
tdef infogr des='infogr'
1/llx = 0 lly = 0
 ulx = 0 uly = 100
 urx =100 ury = 100
 lrx =100 lry = 0
2/llx = 0 lly = 60
 ulx = 0 uly = 82.5
 urx =100 ury = 82.5
 lrx =100 lry = 60
3/llx =32 lly = 38
 ulx =32 uly = 60
 urx =100 ury = 60
 lrx =100 lry = 38
4/llx =32 lly = 9
 ulx =32 uly = 33
 urx =100 ury = 33
 lrx =100 lry = 9
5/llx = 0 lly = 9
 ulx = 0 uly = 33
 urx = 32 ury = 33
 lrx = 32 lry = 9
 ;
```

NOTE PROC GREPLAY

The SAS documentation introduces PROC GPLOT as follows:

The GREPLAY procedure displays and manages graphics output that is stored in SAS catalogs. The GREPLAY procedure also creates templates and color maps that you can use when you replay your graphics output. The GREPLAY procedure operates in line mode, batch mode, interactively in the SAS GUI.

With the GREPLAY procedure, you can perform any of the following actions:

- Layout multiple graphs on one page; this output can be used to create dashboards.
- Select one or more catalog entries from the same catalog for replay, and direct this output to your display or other devices such as plotters and printers.
- Use, create, or modify templates. Use templates to describe positioning on a single display, for graphics output stored in one or more graph catalog entries.
- Create new graphics output by replaying one or more catalog entries into panels within a template.
- Use, create, or modify color maps. Use color maps to map current colors to different colors.
- List templates in SASHELP.TEMPLT.
- Manage GRSEG, TEMPLATE, and CMAP entries in SAS catalogs by doing the following:
- Rearranging or creating logical groupings of catalog entries that contain graphics output.
- Renaming, deleting, or copying catalog entries that contain graphics output, templates, and color maps.

Graphics Output in a Template shows four catalog entries that were replayed into a template and displayed as a single graph.

(For further details, see SAS/GRAPH(R) 9.3: Reference, Third Edition)

Figure 13.2 shows an example of the blank template that is created by the SAS code:

Figure 13.2. SAS Code Infographic: Template Example

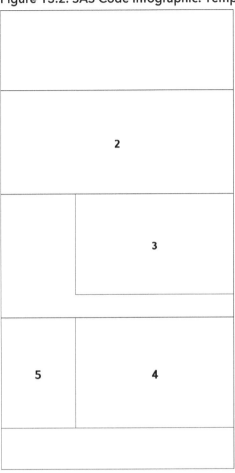

The template is displayed with borders turned on so that you can see the areas. Numbers are used to identify specific locations.

You then replay the grsegs (graphs) into the template. You can specify the area in the GREPLAY template to which the grseg name is assigned:

Program 13.3. Replay the Graphs into the Template

```
template = infogr;
treplay
2:bubble
3:lines
4:map20
5:box20
;
```

Figure 13.3 shows the insertion of the graphs into the template:

Figure 13.3. SAS Code Infographic: Example of a Template with Inserted Graphs

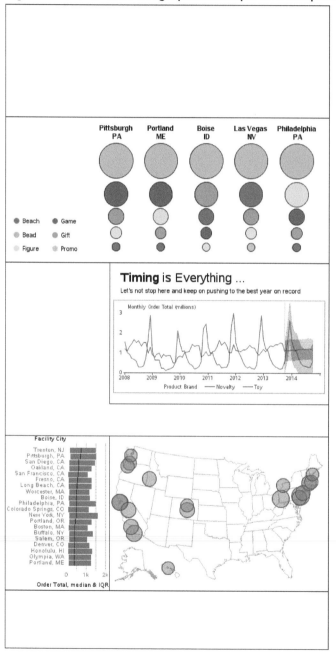

Lastly, you can add some final touches to apply some subjective commentary and images for the visual effect. The final infographic is almost complete, and it is now time to focus on the run time for this SAS program and make this example complete.

Step 4: Run Time

The You can run the SAS code interactively or in batch mode, and you can use a variety of SAS client tools. In this example, we will use SAS Studio to run the SAS code and view the results. This program could also be enhanced to send the output to other formats. SAS Output Delivery System (ODS) includes many predefined options to support Microsoft Excel, PowerPoint, PDF , and EPUB. You could send this file to all of them at once. In this example, we are using HTML (with a PNG file and hover text). Workflow could also be included to enhance the SAS code process. For example, you could email this infographic to interested parties, or specify a network location at which to update the infographic on a regular basis without human intervention.

Figure 13.4 shows the SAS code:

Figure 13.4. Running the SAS Code with SAS Studio

example.sas

CODE LOG RESULTS

```
%let name=Sales_Performance;
filename odsout '.';

/* SAS/Graph Sales Performance Infographic */

libname my_data '.';

/* I just ran this code once, to subset the US data I needed. */
/*
data my_data.va_data_us; set my_data.va_sample_smallinsight
 (where=(FacilityCountryReg='US'));
length statecode $2;
statecode=trim(left(scan(FacilityStateProv,2,'-')));
length facilitycity_state $50;
facilitycity_state=trim(left(facilitycity))||', '||trim(left(statecode));
run;
endsas;
*/

/* turn of displaying of graphics, while you prepare the individual graphs */
goptions nodisplay;

goptions gunit=pct ftitle='albany amt/bold' ftext='albany amt' htitle=3.5 htext=2.5;

/* Define a few macro variables you'll use later ... */

%let metric=ordertotal;

/* general black color, used throughout the dashboard */
%let black=cx002744;

/* Colors for the array of bubbles in the Top 5 plot */
/* (these are assigned alphabetically, based on the productline names) */
%let bubc1=cx4472c4;
%let bubc2=cxfaa743;
%let bubc3=cxede941;
%let bubc4=cx55934a;
%let bubc5=cxf36e42;
%let bubc6=cx8ec8d7;
%let bubc7=cyan;
%let bubc8=magenta;

/* color for colored boxes in the boxplot, and bubbles in the map */
%let boxrgb=007dc3;

/* RGB code for color of the lines & forecast cone, for toy & novelty */
%let toyrgb=ab4f00;
%let novrgb=1d6d74;

/* Month & year, to go in big white ball in top/right (and also used to subset data) */
proc sql noprint;
create table max as select unique max(transactiondate) as maxdate from my_data.va_data_us;
select maxdate format=monname3. into :ytdmon separated by ' ' from max;
select maxdate format=year4. into :ytdyear separated by ' ' from max;
quit; run;

/* Get the most recent year's data */
data va_data_us_thisyear; set my_data.va_data_us
```

C:/Users/sasdemo/Documents/example.sas Line 95, Column 48 UTF-8

Messages: 3 User: sasdemo

When the code is run inside SAS Studio, the generated output is accessible via the **Results** tab. The results show a complete business infographic poster that was created with the SAS code. This example provides a blend of data-driven and non-data content. Figure 13.5:

Figure 13.5. Output of the SAS Program: a Business Infographic Poster

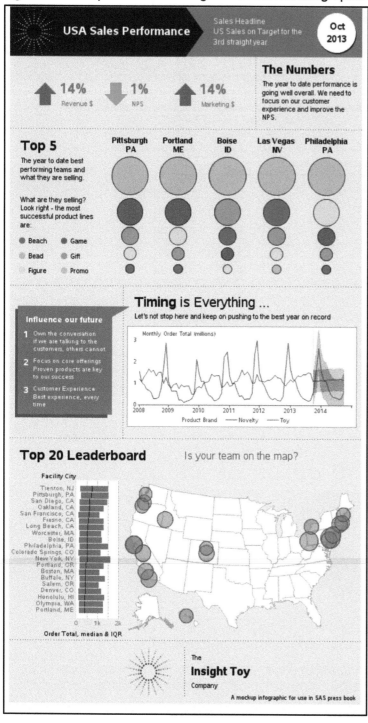

NOTE: Execute your SAS code

Executing the SAS code can be achieved in many ways. In this example, we are using the SAS Studio client to execute the code interactively. We could use another client tool such as SAS Enterprise Guide, to execute this code in batch mode or on-demand. We could also create the code as a SAS Stored Process, which would produce an on-demand custom analytics process to execute by URL.

Example 4.2: Social Media Tiles

Example 4.2 continues with the SAS code to visualize data. This is a simple example of creating an infofragment type of infographic. This example is another approach to leverage SAS to turn your idea into a data-driven analytics process.

Step 1: Design

Creating the design on a whiteboard again is a great way to create without jumping ahead and trying to code first. Also, when you are passing your design to the SAS programmer, the better the mock-up, the less time you spend in the coding stage, especially if you are not the SAS programmer who is writing the code.

Figure 13.6 is an example of the mock-up:

Figure 13.6. Mock-up of the Infofragment with SAS code

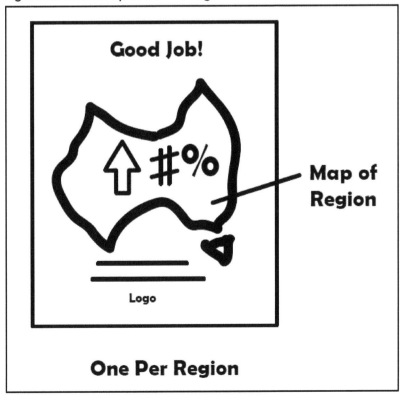

Step 2: Required Elements

Data-Driven Elements

- **Maps** – Each time this is run, you want the map image to change to the correct location that you are focused on at that time.

- **Arrow** – Business rules are driving the behavior of this arrow: up is for positive performers, and down is for lower-than-expected performers.

- **Performance Year on Year** – Each year is assessed individually, and can be changed to make this useful each year.

- **Text** – Static and dynamic text elements are required for your infofragment. Some text (such as year and region) is data-driven. Some text (such as for the heading) is rule-based and is adapted for good and not-so-good performing teams.

Non-Data Driven Elements

- **Logo** – A static image for your logo is used each time.

- **Text** – Some connecting text for your infofragment is not data-driven. It essentially connects the data-driven and business rule-driven text elements together. This creates a data paragraph and places the data-driven text into the correct sentence structure.

To achieve this design, we need some conditional logic that is written into the code to dynamically decide on the data to show and what text to display.

Step 3: Walking through the Code

Because this code example is simpler than the code in the previous example, we can show the full code. Read the comments in the code to understand what is happening in each step.

Program 13.4. SAS Code Sample

```
%let name=map_tile;
filename odsout '.';

/* Set some variables to drive the data selection. */

%let thisyear=2013;
%let prevyear=2012;
%let curdate=30oct;

libname my_data '.';

/* Run this code just once, to make the dataset a bit smaller. */
/*
data my_data.va_data_continent; set my_data.va_sample_smallinsight
  (keep = ordertotal facilitycontinent transactiondate);
run;
endsas;
*/
```

```
%macro do_cont(datacont, mapcont, contname);

proc sql noprint;

/* Calculate ytd revenue for this continent */

create table ytd_current as
select unique facilitycontinent, sum(ordertotal) as current_total
from my_data.va_data_continent
where
facilitycontinent="&datacont" and
transactiondate>="01jan&thisyear"d and
transactiondate<="&curdate&thisyear"d;

/* Calculate previous year's ytd revenue for this continent */

create table ytd_previous as
select unique facilitycontinent, sum(ordertotal) as previous_total
from my_data.va_data_continent
where
facilitycontinent="&datacont" and
transactiondate>="01jan&prevyear"d and
transactiondate<="&curdate&prevyear"d;

quit; run;

/* combine into one dataset, and calculate the % change */

data ytd_data; merge ytd_current ytd_previous;
by facilitycontinent;

percent_change=current_total/previous_total;

length revenue_direction $10;
if percent_change>=1.00 then revenue_direction='up';
else revenue_direction='down';

length percent_text $10;
percent_text=put(abs(percent_change-1),percentn7.0);

length message_text $50;
if percent_change>=1.10 then message_text="Awesome Job Team!";
else if percent_change>=1.00 then message_text="Good Job Team";
else if percent_change<1.00 then message_text="Keep Working Together";
run;

/*
Save the data values into macro variables, such as ...
%let message=Awesome Job!;
%let revdir=up;
%let percent=14%;
*/
```

```
proc sql noprint;
select unique message_text into :message separated by ' ' from ytd_data;
select unique revenue_direction into :revdir separated by ' ' from ytd_data;
select unique percent_text into :percent separated by ' ' from ytd_data;
quit; run;


data anno_stuff;
length function $8 style $35 color $12 text $100;
xsys='3'; ysys='3'; hsys='3';

/* annotate a different colored background for each continent */

when='b';
if "&datacont"='NA' then color="cx55934a"; /* green */
if "&datacont"='SA' then color="cxf36e42"; /* orange */
if "&datacont"='EU' then color="cx007dc3"; /* blue */
if "&datacont"='OC' then color="cxb72a2b"; /* dark red */
if "&datacont"='AS' then color="cxede941"; /* yellow */
if "&datacont"='AF' then color="cx8ec8d7"; /* light blue */
x=0; y=0; function='move'; output;
x=100; y=100; function='box'; style='solid'; line=0; output;
x=0; y=0; function='move'; output;
x=100; y=100; function='box'; style='empty'; line=0; color="gray55"; output;


color=''; when='a';

function='label';

/* Revenue % up/down arrow */

x=42; y=55;
size=17; position='4'; style="Wingdings 3";
if "&revdir"="up" then text="c7"x;
else if "&revdir"="down" then text="c8"x;
output;

/* Revenue percent (beside the arrow) */

x=x+4; y=55;
size=17; position='6'; style="albany amt/bold";
text="&percent";
output;

/* Text below map */

position='5'; size=4.5;
x=50;
y=23; text="The year to date sales for"; output;
y=y-6; text="&contname are &revdir for &thisyear"; output;

/* text for company logo at bottom */

x=50; position='6'; color="black";
y=9.8; size=2.5; style="albany amt"; text="The"; output;
y=7.0; size=3.0; style="albany amt/bold"; text="Insight Toy"; output;
y=3.2; size=2.5; style="albany amt"; text="Company"; output;
```

```
/* image for company logo at bottom */
x=33; y=1; function='move'; output;
x=48; y=11.5; function='image'; imgpath='logo.png'; style='fit'; output;

run;

/* Trim off some of the extreme outlier regions of the maps,
 to get visually better 'continent' continent maps.
*/
data my_map other; set mapsgfk.&mapcont (where=(density<=2) drop=resolution);
if x^=. and
 (
 "&datacont"='NA' and x<-.7 /* Alaska */
 or
 "&datacont"='NA' and x>0.5 /* Some of the Caribbean Islands */
 or
 "&datacont"='SA' and x<-2000 /* Galapagos Islands */
 or
 "&datacont"='EU' and x<-.3 /* Canary Islands, etc */
or
 "&datacont"='EU' and y>.35 /* Islands north of Europe */
 or
 "&datacont"='OC' and x>.39 /* Some Pacific Islands */
 or
 "&datacont"='OC' and y>.2 /* Some Pacific Islands */
 or
 "&datacont"='AF' and x<-.65 /* Islands west of Africa */
 or
 "&datacont"='AF' and x>.62 /* Islands east of Africa */
 )
 then output other;
else output my_map;
run;

goptions gunit=pct ftitle='albany amt/bold' ftext='albany amt' htitle=3.5 htext=2.5;
goptions ctext=white;

pattern1 v=s c=Affffff22;

/* Make some blank space to annotate things into */

title1 h=7pct ls=1.5 "&message";
footnote h=20pct " ";

proc gmap data=my_map map=my_map anno=anno_stuff;
id id segment;
choro segment / levels=1 nolegend
 coutline=gray55
 des='' name="&name..&datacont";
run;

%mend;
```

```
goptions device=png;
goptions noborder;
goptions xpixels=400 ypixels=500;

ODS LISTING CLOSE;
ODS HTML path=odsout body="&name..htm"
  (title="Sales by Continent") style=htmlblue;

options mprint;

%do_cont(EU,europe,Europe);
%do_cont(AS,asia,Asia);
%do_cont(NA,namerica,North America);
%do_cont(SA,samerica,South America);
%do_cont(OC,oceania,Oceania);
%do_cont(AF,africa,Africa);


quit;
ODS HTML CLOSE;
ODS LISTING;
```

Step 4: Run Time

We can now run the code inside SAS Studio. The SAS code is formatted to make it easy to read for the SAS programmer. One SAS program was written to create unique infographic per continent within our sales data (see Figure 13.7). The code can automate your process and send an update each time this script is run on the latest data each week, month, quarter, as needed. You could get more sophisticated and post this to your social network with some additional SAS code.

Figure 13.7. Final Output of SAS Code for the Visualization to Social Media Tiles

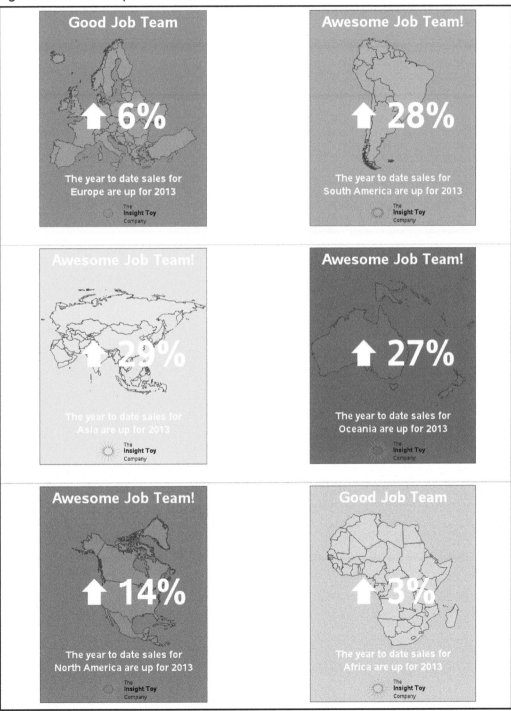

Figure 13.8. Detail of Final Results for the Social Media Tile for the Europe Sales Team

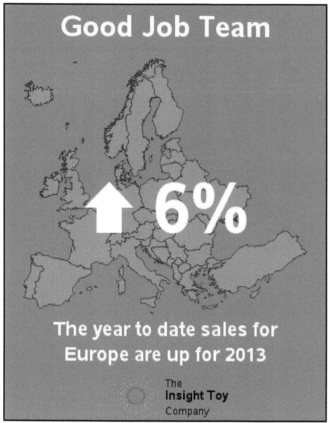

Examples Gallery

Other examples of creating infographics with SAS code are shown in Figures 13.9–13.17 to show you what others have achieved with SAS. Many other examples are available online from SAS experts. However, many of the examples are reproductions of other examples on the internet and in other publications. The infographics in this collection have been re-created and improved, and are available for all to try online. I encourage you to refer to the further reading section and investigate coding in SAS to produce your own infographics. Figures 13.9–13.17 are some examples of using SAS for infographics:

Figure 13.9. Example 1: Using SGPLOT and Some Simple Images to Create Infographic Charts (Image credit: S. Mantage, 2016)

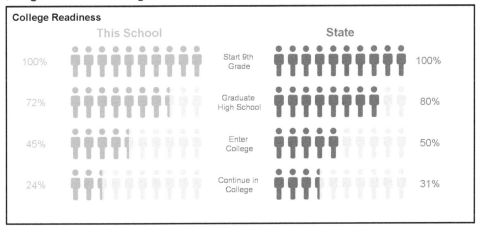

Figure 13.10. Example 2: Coin Infographic Using Images for Bars (Image credit: S. Matange, 2016)

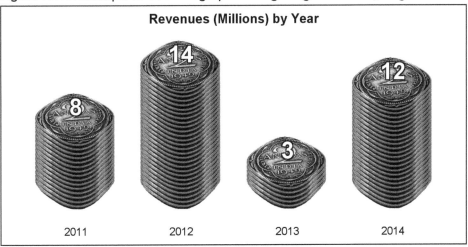

Figure 13.11. Example 3: SAS ODS Graphics Icons with Data Graphics (Image credit: S. Matange, 2016)

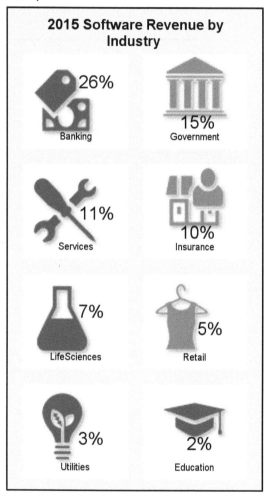

Figure 13.12. Example 4: SAS Global Forum Infographic Example (Image Credit: R. Allison, 2018)

2017 SAS GLOBAL FORUM Attendance and Demographics

Registration

5,182 Attendees

Region

8% Canada

74% US

11% EMEA

4% Asia Pacific

3% Latin America

Industry

24% Services

15% Health Care, Pharma and Life Sciences

6% Manufacturing

18% Banking and Financial Services

6% Government

5% Retail

18% Education

6% Communications

2% Energy and Utilities

Sample Job Functions

15% Data Science

5% Risk

3% CRM/Database Marketing

14% Information Services

4% Finance

2% Engineering

6% Research & Development

4% Medical/Health Care

1% Development Research

6% Education

4% Operations

21% Other

Job Titles

24% Executives

20% Managers

56% Technical Professionals

Sample Job Titles

Executive

Chief Data Officers
Chief Analytics Officers
Chief Executive Officers
Chief Financial Officers
Chief Information Officers

Analytics Directors and Managers
Global Business Development Executives
Executive Directors of Marketing Analytics
Chief Medical Officers
Chief Operating Officers

Executive Vice Presidents
Chief Technology Officers

Technical

Data Scientists
Data Analysts
BI Specialists
Statisticians
Biostatisticians
Operations Managers

Quality Engineers
Consultants
Programmers
IT Specialists
Marketing Analysts
Project Managers

Business Analysts
Data Architects
Data Consultants
Database Administrators

Figure 13.13. Example 5: Pretty Maps with SAS Code. SAS/GRAPH Provides a Grid of Dots (Image Credit: R. Allison, 2015)

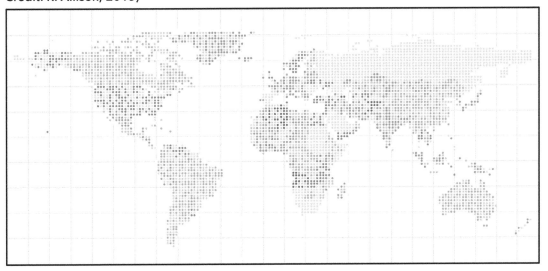

Figure 13.14. Example 6: One SAS Program Creates Many Infographics Based on the Data (Image credit: R. Allison, 2015)

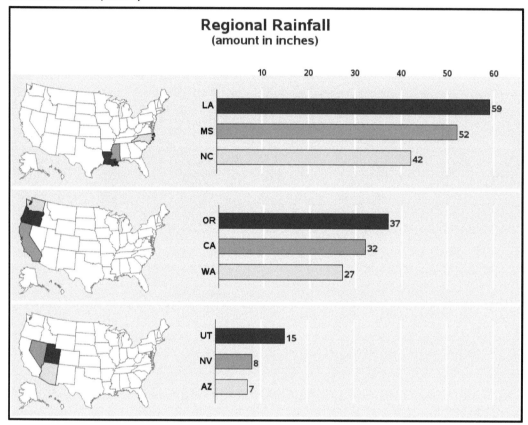

Figure 13.15. Example 7: Floor Plan Infographic. Applying Data to the Floorplan of a Theatre to Compare Performance against any Metric (Such as Profit, Popularity, and Availability) (Image credit: R. Allison, 2015)

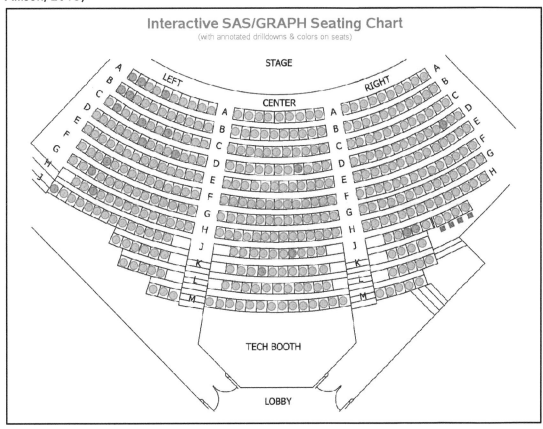

Figure 13.16. Example 8: Simple Infofragment Using a Headline to Reinforce the Data-Driven Visuals (Image credit: R. Allison, 2015)

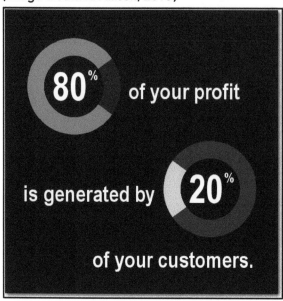

Figure 13.17. Example 9: Doomsday Infographic Example using SAS Code to Get a Point Across (Image credit: R. Allison, 2015)

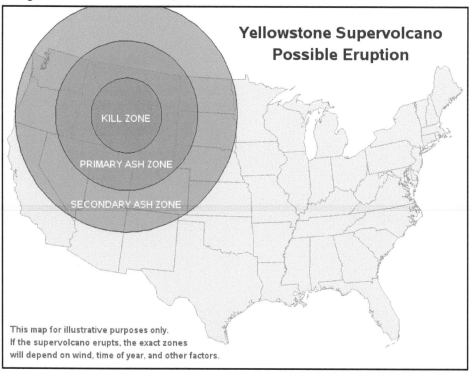

Where to Go from Here?

Overview

In this chapter, we look at planning where to go from here, and to highlight that the learning continues, and that the software is forever changing. It is the reader's challenge to stay informed and aware of the latest changes in SAS software. This last chapter sets a vision for emerging trends and potential tools and technologies to influence the next generation of business infographics that are powered by SAS. As SAS continues to innovate in data visualization and analytics with regular updates to the software offerings used in this book, more power is being introduced in this area all the time. Staying ahead of the curve is always a challenge.

Audience

All levels of SAS users will find this chapter of interest.

Which Approach Do I Choose?

Of the options outlined in the examples, you can choose to use the one that fits the project that you have in mind. I get asked often to show how SAS can do infographics, and I always say to define the project's objective first. For example, if the emphasis is on the ease of creation of the infographic, then I recommend using SAS Visual Analytics to help develop a prototype to share with the team who is asking for it. They will quickly point out the things that they like and dislike using the simple drag-and-drop interface of SAS Visual Analytics. Often their requirements will solidify during this process, and you can gauge whether pixel-perfect design is the goal. Once you have clarity on this requirement, you quickly learn which option will best meet your project's needs. What I think is important to note here is the benefits of using SAS to step through each stage of your analysis and design process.

All examples shown illustrate creating infographics. However, as you see in Figure 14.1, the benefits are that all options leverage data and computations from the SAS Analytics Platform.

Figure 14.1. All Options, Same Platform

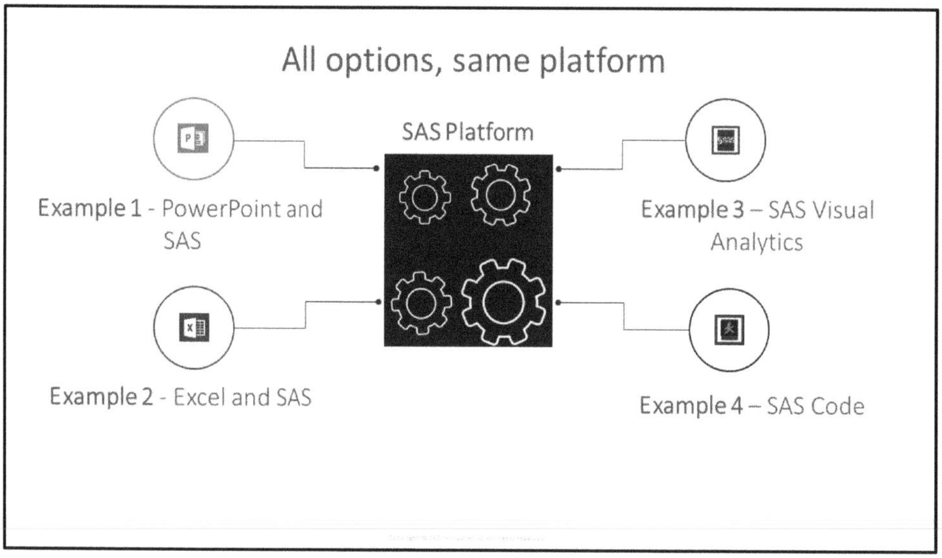

Pathways and Training Resources

It is not enough to gain access to simple yet powerful software, such as SAS Visual Analytics. You need to get instruction and techniques to use that software to achieve your tasks and to spot opportunities to apply it.

In my dealings with customers, I am often asked the same questions about SAS Visual Analytics, and when I finish answering these, the customer nearly always says "I wish I had known that earlier. It could have saved me so much time doing ...". This has prompted me to share some resources to help you understand SAS and all its functional glory, and to empower you to get the most from your investment.

Many people purchase SAS Visual Analytics for a particular use case. They have an immediate business problem and learn just enough to solve that problem. Rarely do they learn more than is necessary initially. Without a broader understanding of the capabilities of their software, when the next business challenge surfaces, they might not know that SAS could also solve that challenge. Infographics might the next area that you use SAS software for.

Another situation that we encounter at our customer sites is staff changeover in personnel that purchased SAS software. Often, business units get told that they now have this great new software from SAS that is available for use. This is great! However, at the core of "getting the most from your software" is developing the skills to go with that software, which often occurs via trial and error. Reading this book is a step in that direction to help with your learning curve with SAS software.

Through my years of using many vendors' software, I believe that the knowledge that I have gained about the less obvious features of certain software has provided me with many benefits that I can share across organizations.

I've scoured the globe (well, the internet) to find available resources that I think will help you learn about SAS Visual Analytics and all that it offers. Below are the best sources of knowledge to start your skills development with SAS, and you'll find even more listed in the bibliography:

Free Video Library
http://video.sas.com/#category/videos/sas-visual-analytics

This resource contains simple "how to" videos that range in length from two to ten minutes. These are bite-sized videos that focus on completing a particular task in SAS such as loading data and navigating the application. This is a great resource for those who need a quick refresher as a follow-up to training course or those who need to learn SAS "just in time" to complete a task today. The videos are organized by different functional areas, and also include introduction and getting started tutorials.

"Ask the Experts" Series

https://support.sas.com/training/askexpert.html

This is a great resource for comprehensive video content that is delivered in webisode format. Webinar style videos can be subscribed to either as live sessions or on-demand. This is a great way to learn and is a step farther than the other resources in this section. I particularly like this resource because you get exposure to a wide range of people with different experiences with SAS software. This range of knowledge makes the learning particularly rich. It provides a deep dive into a particular topic, and it provides more context than a short video can. You can learn from the experts without leaving your desk.

SAS YouTube Channel

https://www.youtube.com/user/SASsoftware

The SAS YouTube channel is a treasure trove of amazing software demonstrations and webinar content that shows the power of SAS. We are using YouTube more and more to share the best practices of using SAS software. If you are like me, you will find this channel to be a fun place to watch your favorite SAS experts share their tips and tricks with you.

This channel is a great place to see industry examples and applications of SAS that solve specific problems. It doesn't just show software features and functions. This channel contains more end-to-end examples of SAS in the real world in bite-size servings, which run mostly under ten minutes and give you great value. Another great reason to visit this channel is to hear stories about customers and how they achieve success with SAS. You hear directly from the source.

This is only a sample of what is available on the internet for self-paced learning and skills development with your SAS software.

Of course, once you master these free channels for learning SAS, you can take your skills to the next level with online and classroom training programs at https://support.sas.com/training/ and SAS certification programs at https://www.sas.com/certification to really know the software and all it offers you and your business. So, remember that investing some time for you and your team on the capabilities of SAS will enable you to spot the next business opportunity while leveraging your software.

Future Trends

The goal of this section of the book is to predict trends for the future of data visualization. Here are my top emerging trends for the coming year in data visualization and analytics:

Open

"Open" does not just mean open source. In fact, many of the open-source data analysis and data visualization tools will fall away while new ones will rise, and some will continue to improve. The challenges for enterprises are the niche use cases and the skills that are required to use each of these offerings. The SAS roadmap shows a continuation of what was started with the SAS platform. It extends and embraces more platforms to ensure that the benefits of the SAS analytics engine are available to other tools such as R, Python, Java, Lua, and REST APIs.

"Open" also extends to curated open and public data sets for the world to use to solve complex problems. These open resources will then be available to many more people who can tell stories and share insights.

Ubiquitous Data Visualization

The tides have turned, and in the next one to two years, we will see even more approachable data-driven communication in the broader market place. SAS capabilities continue to innovate and focus on visual capability in solutions, such as SAS Visual Analytics, to highlight and communicate value from analytics.

Motion Infographics

Animated and multi-frame visualizations will grow in use and ease of creation as the volume of data increases and the appetite for data visualization increases. More motion will be added to clarify the infographic without audio or context from a presenter or SME. This might also move us more into augmented reality with data visualization, especially if technical implementations of augmented reality become mainstream.

Massive Data

I can't even use the term "big data" anymore. It is just back to data and new data sources from here on. To reiterate a statement from Dr. Goodnight, CEO of SAS, at SAS Global Forum 2017, "Data is your fuel, and analytics is your engine."

Data is everywhere, and with this data the story that we tell becomes even more important. Adding context and driving action and insight is growing as was the case over the past decades. Ubiquitous access to core data sources will continue to be a core requirement for data visualization.

Real-Time Infographics

Similar to operational dashboards in the power plant or the manufacturing floor, infographics with streamed feeds from data is on the rise. The advent of the Internet of Things (IoT) and analytics at the edge will also need data visualization. SAS is invested heavily in this area with event stream processing capabilities to analyze the data in the stream and to update downstream flows and processes.

Age of Automation

For many industries, automation drives digital disruption around the globe. This is also true for data visualization. Use of bots will grow to automatically create and distribute engaging snippets of data visuals to users. Machine-assisted data visuals will continue to evolve and drive innovation in many aspects of self-service analytics and infographics.

Crowd Sourcing / Data for Good

These might be separate items but the sharing of expertise will be a hallmark of the next few years in data visualization. SAS launched GatherIQ (https://gatheriq.analytics/) to connect analysts with interesting data projects and to host open and curated data sets. Analytics skills as well as custom data visualization and infographic skills will be in demand to achieve the goals of "Data for Good". So, make a difference and volunteer your skills today, whether you are a data artist or a data scientist.

Hyper-Personalization

Customers are being treated as a unique person like never before, and personalized infographics will be available that apply personal context for that single customer along with those unique behaviors. The online world will feel more customized for the individual than ever before based on the data visuals and infographics that are being displayed.

Evolution of Personal Productivity

New and improved tools continue to change the way we work, and SAS is also working to adapt to these reimagined tools in personal productivity. Cloud services such as Microsoft Office 365 and Google Docs will continue to remove the desktop dependence and make the experience consistent no matter where you use it or what device you are using.

These are all happening today. However, I feel that the points that I made above will continue to make an impact on the data visualization landscape more than ever over the next few years. I will check back with this list to see whether that, in fact, actually happens.

Closing Comment

Here is a final comment on this book and the goals I aimed to achieve.

The aim of this book was to introduce a new use case for your trusted software from SAS, specifically SAS Visual Analytics and SAS Office Analytics. I hope that this book has provided some ideas about how you could adopt and achieve data-driven visualization in your business. I hope that a step-by-step guide to create business infographics with SAS generates some ideas and helps you put these into action. I encourage you to share your creations and experiences with the SAS Visual Analytics user community site at communities.sas.com.

Remember that infographics and data visualizations need to include the narrative or the context in order to meet the needs of the audience. It's not just about the aesthetics. I also note that some of my worked examples go beyond my recommendations to you because I wanted to include some additional functionality and user options to show you the "art of the possible" with SAS software. You can have repeatable infographics with restricted access to analytics resources within your enterprise. This leverages the power of big data and the SAS analytics engine with your familiar Microsoft Office productivity tools that you use every day. Thanks for taking the time to come down this path with me. Let's keep on telling these stories with data.

Bibliography

Aanderud, Tricia, Rob Collum, and Ryan Kumpfmiller. (2017). An Introduction to SAS Visual Analytics: How to Explore Numbers, Design Reports and Gain Insight into Your Data. Cary, NC: SAS Institute, Inc.

Allison, Robert. (2012). *SAS/GRAPH: Beyond the Basics.* Cary, NC: SAS Institute Inc.

Allison, Robert. (2013). Creating fancy 'infographics' with SAS. 2013. Robert Allison. Available at http://blogs.sas.com/content/sastraining/2013/04/11/creating-fancy-infographics-with-sas/ (accessed March 22, 2018).

Allison, Robert. (2014). Creating 'pretty' maps with SAS. Available at http://blogs.sas.com/content/sastraining/2014/01/08/creating-pretty-maps-with-sas (accessed March 21, 2018).

Allison, Robert. (2015). When art and analytics collide. Available at http://blogs.sas.com/content/sastraining/2015/03/24/when-art-and-analytics-collide (accessed March 21, 2018).

Allison, Robert. (2015). Robert Allison's SAS/GRAPH InfoGraphics! Available at http://robslink.com/SAS/democd_infographics/aaaindex.htm (accessed March 22, 2018).

Allison, Robert. (2018). Building a SAS Global Forum Infographic. Available at https://blogs.sas.com/content/sastraining/2018/02/14/building-a-sas-global-forum-infographic/ (accessed March 21, 2018).

Allison, Robert. (n.d.). Robert Allison's SAS/Graph Samples #48. Available at http://robslink.com/SAS/democd48/theater_info.htm (accessed March 21, 2018).

Allison, Robert. (n.d.). Robert Allison's SAS/Graph Samples #52. Available at http://robslink.com/SAS/democd52/micromaps_info.htm (accessed March 21, 2018).

Allison, Robert. (n.d.). Robert Allison's SAS/Graph Samples #70. Available at http://robslink.com/SAS/democd70/yellowstone_supervolcano_info.htm (accessed March 21, 2018).

Allison, Robert. (n.d.). Robert Allison's SAS/GRAPH Examples! Available at http://robslink.com/SAS/ (accessed March 21, 2018).

Allison, Robert. (n.d.). The Graph Guy! Available at http://blogs.sas.com/content/author/robertallison/ (accessed February 22, 2018).

Bailey, David., Anand Chitale, and I-Kong Fu. (2014). Share Your SAS® Visual Analytics Reports with SAS® Office Analytics. Proceedings of the SAS Global Forum 2014 Conference. Cary, NC: SAS Institute, Inc. Available at http://support.sas.com/resources/papers/proceedings14/SAS274-2014.pdf (accessed March 22, 2018).

Bailey, David, Tim Beese, and Casey Smith. (2015). Take Your Data Analysis and Reporting to the Next Level by Combining SAS® Office Analytics, SAS® Visual Analytics, and SAS® Studio. Proceedings of the SAS

Global Forum 2015 Conference. Cary, NC: SAS Institute Inc. Available at https://support.sas.com/resources/papers/proceedings15/SAS1804-2015.pdf (accessed March 22, 2018).

Beese, Tim. (2016). Building Interactive Microsoft Excel Worksheets with SAS Office Analytics. Proceedings of the SAS Global Forum 2016 Conference. Cary, NC: SAS Institute Inc. Available at http://support.sas.com/resources/papers/proceedings16/SAS3500-2016.pdf (accessed March 22, 2018).

Cody, Ron. (2015). *An Introduction to SAS University Edition*. Cary, NC: SAS Institute Inc.

Dale, Edgar. (1969). *Audio-Visual Methods in Teaching*, 3rd ed. New York: Holt, Rinehart & Winston.

Der, Geoff and Brian S. Everitt. (2015). *Essential Statistics Using SAS University Edition*. Cary, NC: SAS Institute Inc.

Farnsworth, A. (2017). How the British Broadcasting Corporation Uses Data to Tell Stories in a Visually Compelling Way. SAS Global Forum 2017. Available at: http://video.sas.com/sasgf17/detail/videos/user-program/video/5383562321001/how-the-british-broadcasting-corporation-uses-data-to-tell-stories-in-a-visually-compelling-way (accessed March 21, 2018).

Few, Stephan. 2006. *Information Dashboard Design*. Sebastopol, CA: O'Reilly Media.

Encyclopedia Britannica Online. (2015). Moore's law. Available at: https://www.britannica.com/technology/Moores-law (accessed October 9, 2017).

Just, Marcel, and Melissa Ludtke. 2010. Watching the Human Brain Process Information. Available at http://niemanreports.org/articles/watching-the-human-brain-process-information/ (accessed March 21, 2018).

Krum, Randy. (2014). *Cool Infographics: Effective Communication with Data Visualization and Design*. New York: Wiley.

Matange, Sanjay. (2016). Infographics using SAS. Available at http://blogs.sas.com/content/graphicallyspeaking/2016/02/10/infographics (accessed October 9, 2017).

Matange, Sanjay. (2016). Infographics Bar Chart. Available at: http://blogs.sas.com/content/graphicallyspeaking/2016/02/18/infographics-bar-chart/ (accessed October 9, 2017).

Matange, Sanjay. (2016). Infographics: Coin Stack Bar Chart. Available at http://blogs.sas.com/content/graphicallyspeaking/2016/06/12/infographics-coin-stacks (accessed October 9, 2017).

Matange, Sanjay. (2016). Outside-the-Box: Directed circle link graphs. Available at http://blogs.sas.com/content/graphicallyspeaking/2016/11/01/outside-box-directed-circle-link-graphs/ (accessed October 9, 2017).

Matange, Sanjay. (2017). Lollipop Charts. Available at http://blogs.sas.com/content/graphicallyspeaking/2017/07/24/lollipop-charts/(accessed October 9, 2017).

Merieb, Elaine N., and Katja Hoehn. 2007. *Human Anatomy & Physiology*, 7th ed. San Francisco, CA: Benjamin Cummings.

Mckinsey Global Institute. (2016). The Age of Analytics: Competing in a Data-driven World. Available at http://www.mckinsey.com/business-functions/mckinsey-analytics/our-insights/the-age-of-analytics-competing-in-a-data-driven-world (accessed March 22, 2018).

McSpadden, Kevin. 2015. You Now Have a Shorter Attention Span Than a Goldfish. Available at http://time.com/3858309/attention-spans-goldfish/ (accessed March 21, 2018).

Murphy, T. and Falko Schulz. 2018. Supercharge Your Dashboards with Infographic Concepts Using SAS® Visual Analytics. Proceedings of the SAS Global Forum 2018 Conference. Cary, NC: SAS Institute Inc.

Available at: http://support.sas.com/resources/papers/proceedings16/SAS3360-2016.pdf (accessed March 22, 2018).

Narechania, A. (2017). Condegram Spiral Plot. Available at https://bl.ocks.org/arpitnarechania/027e163073864ef2ac4ceb5c2c0bf616 (accessed October 9, 2017).

SAS Institute (2014). Create a Stored Process from a Single Task. Cary, NC: SAS Institute, Inc. Available at http://video.sas.com/detail/videos/how-to-tutorials/video/3829689285001/create-a-stored-process-from-a-single-task (accessed September 21, 2017).

SAS Institute (2017). SAS/GRAPH online documentation. Cary, NC: SAS Institute, Inc. Available at http://go.documentation.sas.com/api/docsets/graphref/9.4/content/graphref.pdf?locale=en#nameddest=titlepage (accessed March 22, 2018).

SAS Institute Inc. (2015). SAS® Visual Analytics: User's Guide. Cary, NC: SAS Institute Inc. Available at http://support.sas.com/documentation/cdl/en/vaug/67500/PDF/default/vaug.pdf (accessed March 22, 2018).

SAS Institute Inc. (2016). SAS® Office Analytics Fact Sheet. Cary, NC: SAS Institute Inc. Available at https://www.sas.com/content/dam/SAS/en_us/doc/factsheet/sas-office-analytics-105595.pdf (accessed March 22, 2018).

SAS Institute Inc. (n.d.). SAS Visual Analytics Community. SAS Support Communities. Cary, NC: SAS Institute Inc. Available at https://communities.sas.com/community/support-communities/sas-visual-analytics (accessed March 22, 2018).

SAS Institute Inc. (n.d.). SAS® Visual Analytics: Video Library. Cary, NC: SAS Institute Inc. Available at http://support.sas.com/training/tutorial/va73/ (accessed March 22, 2018).

SAS Institute, Inc. (n.d). SAS Graphically Speaking Blog. Available at: http://blogs.sas.com/content/graphicallyspeaking/ (accessed March 22, 2018).

SAS Institute, Inc. (n.d). Getting Started with SAS Studio. Available at http://video.sas.com/detail/videos/sas-studio/video/4573016757001/getting-started-with-sas-studio (accessed on February 22, 2018).

SAS Institute, Inc. (n.d). Data Can be Beautiful. Available at: http://support.sas.com/rnd/report-design-best-practice/index.html (accessed March 22, 2018).

Schulz, Falko. (2017). How to design an infographic about volcanic eruptions using SAS Visual Analytics. Available at http://blogs.sas.com/content/sascom/2017/04/10/design-infographic-volcanic-eruptions-using-sas-visual-analytics (accessed October 10, 2017).

Schulz, Falko. (2017). How to design a meteorite infographic using NASA data and SAS. Available at: http://blogs.sas.com/content/sascom/2017/03/28/design-meteorite-infographic-using-nasa-data-sas (accessed October 9, 2017).

Semetko, Holli, and Margaret Scammell. (2012). *The SAGE Handbook of Political Communication*. Thousand Oaks, CA: SAGE Publications.

Shaw, Ray. (2017). Data without analytics is data not yet realised (interview). ITWIRE. Available at: https://www.itwire.com/data/77711-data-without-analytics-is-data-not-yet-realised-interview.html (accessed March 21, 2018).

Ternouth, Martin. (n.d.). Edward Tufte forum: Pie Charts. Available at https://www.edwardtufte.com/bboard/q-and-a-fetch-msg?msg_id=00018S (accessed October 9, 2017).

Tukey, John. W. (1977). *Exploratory Data Analysis*. Reading, MA: Addison-Wesley.

Turner, Mike. (2017). Hyperpersonalisation: What does it mean for your customers? Available at: http://players.brightcove.net/1872491364001/default_default/index.html?videoId=5400785710001 (accessed March 22, 2018).

The Data – Why this Data? (Sample Data)

Data Overview

In this book, the sales data is focused on a fictitious toy company and has been shipped with SAS Visual Analytics in earlier releases. This focus enables you to maximize your efforts as you consider the visual elements. Also, many organizations are driven by metrics such as profit, revenue, and costs, which makes this use case relevant for many readers.

This data choice could make some readers sigh, thinking "more fake sales data for some made-up company", and you are heard loud and clear. The reason to choose and stick with a simple and familiar data set is that this book aims to show a repeatable approach to use on your own data. The more familiar you become with the approach and the simpler it is to try for yourself, the more likely you are to learn from the examples. This data also helps the book be approachable for people in all stages of their SAS skills journey.

I hope you see the benefits of using a simple data set throughout this book. The book is about what is possible with your data. I am always frustrated when I see worked examples in software books that use exotic data sets that are located on a remote web page and that the reader to do the work on the data context, data preparation, and information design. Based on your feedback to this book, I am receptive to the idea of including more data in future updates, especially because the sample data that is shipped with SAS evolves across releases.

Data Location

Grab the data from SAS press page (VA_SAMPLE_SMALLINSIGHT.sas7bat). Located at this link:

http://support.sas.com/murphy

The following table shows the data dictionary that corresponds with the sample data that is used in this book.

Table A.1. Sample Data: Data Dictionary

Name	Role	Description
Facility	Geography/ Category	Unique identifier of the selling facility
Facility City	Geography/ Category	City where the selling facility is located
Facility Continents	Geography/ Category	Continent where the selling facility is located
Facility Country/Region	Geography/ Category	Country where the selling facility is located
Facility Country/Region Code	Geography/ Category	Country where the selling facility is located
Facility State/Province	Geography/ Category	State or Province where the selling facility is located
Manufacturing Facility	Geography/ Category	Identifier and location of the manufacturing facility
Order	Category	Order ID
Product Brand	Category	2 product brands: "Novelty" and "Toy".
Product Line	Category	8 product lines. A line belongs to one product brand (see above)
Product Make	Category	77 product make, falling into the 8 product lines.71 product makes. A make belongs to one product line (see above).
Product SKU	Category	779 product SKUs produced, falling into the various product styles

Name	Role	Description
Product Style	Category	335 product styles. A style belongs to one product make (see above).
Sales Rep	Category	ID of the sales representative that made the sale.
Transaction Date	Date	Date of the sale, from January 1st, 1998 to December 31st, 2012.
Transaction Day of Week	Date	Day of the week when the sale happened ("Monday", "Tuesday", and so on).
Transaction Month of Year	Date	Month and year of the sale, from January 1998 to December 2012.
Vendor	Category	Vendor ID
Vendor Loyalty Program	Category	Yes or No - part of our loyalty scheme
market penetration	Measure	For each transaction, the corresponding % of market share in that particular region at that time.
Order Distribution Cost	Measure	Distribution cost associated with that transaction
Order Marketing Cost	Measure	Marketing cost assigned to that transaction (through an activity-based costing exercise)
Order Product Cost	Measure	Direct manufacturing costs associated with that transaction. Included I the calculation of gross Margin.
Order Sales Cost	Measure	Sales-related costs assigned to that transaction (through an activity-based costing exercise)
Order Total	Measure	Revenue from that sale.
Sales Rep % of Target	Measure	A ratio of Sales Rep Actual sales divided by Sales Rep target. Calculated DAILY

Name	Role	Description
Sales Rep Actual	Measure	Cumulative DAILY sales for each sales representative. This value should not be summed across the transactions (since it has already been aggregated).
Sales Rep Orders	Measure	Number of orders a sales representative is responsible for on each date.
Sales Rep Rating	Measure	The internal organization's evaluation of the performance of a sales representative.
Sales Rep Target	Measure	Daily sales Target (goal) for each sales representative. This value should not be summed across the transactions (since it has already been aggregated).
Sales Rep Vendor Base	Measure	Potential revenue (funnel) from all the vendors (customers) assigned to a sales representative. This value should not be summed across the transactions (since it has already been aggregated).
Sales Rep Vendors	Measure	Number of customers (vendors) assigned to a sales representative. This value should not be summed across the transactions (since it has already been aggregated).
Vendor Distance	Measure	Distance from the vendor location to our selling facility.
Vendor Rating	Measure	Subjective evaluation, from 0% to 100%, representing the potential value of a customer (vendor) for insight Toy.
Vendor Satisfaction	Measure	Satisfaction of the customer (vendor) based on a marketing survey. From 0% to 100%.
vendor type	Measure	5 types of vendors: Convenience store, Department store, Kiosk or Other. 1-5 (see user created below)

Name	Role	Description
Xyfacility city lat	Measure	Latitude
Xyfacility city lon	Measure	Longitude
Xyfacility continent lat	Measure	Latitude of continent
Xyfacility continent lon	Measure	Longitude of continent
Xyfacility Country/Region lat	Measure	Latitude of region
Xyfacility Country/Region lon	Measure	Longitude of region
Xyfacility Facility lat	Measure	Latitude of facility
Xyfacility Facility lon	Measure	Longitude of facility
Xyfacility Facility State/Province lat	Measure	Latitude of state
Xyfacility Facility State/Province lon	Measure	Longitude of state
Xy Manufacturing Facility lat	Measure	Latitude of production facility
Xy Manufacturing Facility lon	Measure	Longitude of production facility
Xy Vendor lat	Measure	Latitude of customer location
XY Vendor lon	Measure	Longitude of customer location

Data Enrichment

For the examples in this book, some additional steps are provided when using the data in SAS Visual Analytics. These additional steps include the simple drag-and-drop features in SAS Visual Analytics to enhance and prepare the data on your dashboards. You do not need to prepare the data before you load it into SAS Visual Analytics.

Geographic Data Items

To change a category to a geospatial data item, you simply edit the data item by changing the type option to **Geography** and then complete the wizard-based prompts. Change the type option for the following data items:

- Continent (custom) using latitude and longitude
- Country (custom) using latitude and longitude

- Facility (custom) using latitude and longitude
- Sales City (custom) using latitude and longitude
- Sales Country (ISO 2-letter Country code) using system set values
- Vendor (custom) using latitude and longitude

Other Data Items

Use the following definitions to create some additional data items in SAS Visual Analytics to support the examples in this book.

The following tables contain definitions that were used to create additional data items.

Table A.2. Sample Data: Definitions for Hierarchies

Name	Role	Description	Notes
Geo Hierarchy	Hierarchy	A custom hierarchy made up of Facility, City, State, Country, Continent.	User-Created
Product Hierarchy	Hierarchy	A custom hierarchy made up of Product SKU, Style, Make, Line and Brand	User-Created

Table A.3. Sample Data: Definitions for Calculations

Name	Role	Description	Notes
Gross Margin Ratio	Aggregated Measure	Sum of Gross Margins divided by Sum of Sales ('Order Total')	User-Created
Gross Margin	Measure	Gross Margin for each Sale = 'Order Total' – 'Order Product Cost'	User-Created
Frequency	Measure	Sum of Tows in Table	System-Generated

Table A.4. Sample Data: Definitions for Aggregated Calculations

Name	Role	Description	Notes
Frequency Percent	Measure	% aggregation of the frequency column that has been renamed in some examples as 'Market Share'	System-Generated

Table A.5. Sample Data: Definitions for Custom Category

Name	Role	Description	Notes
Vendor Type	Original column Vendor type	Mapped values 1=Kiosk, 2= online, 3= shopfront, 4= ??, 5=	
Continents Desc	Continents	Description of Continents where values are re-coded to the names of continents. (This changes the codes for the labels to display). Values are re-coded on-the- ly.	

Table A.6. Sample Data: Definitions for Duplicated Data Items

Original Name	New Name	Format
Transaction Date	Transaction Date: Month and Year	MMMYYYY
Transaction Date	Transaction Date: Month - Year	MMYYYY

Index

Ready to take your SAS® and JMP® skills up a notch?

Be among the first to know about new books,
special events, and exclusive discounts.
support.sas.com/newbooks

Share your expertise. Write a book with SAS.
support.sas.com/publish

sas.com/books
for additional books and resources.

THE POWER TO KNOW®

CPSIA information can be obtained
at www.ICGtesting.com
Printed in the USA
LVHW02s0759240418
574597LV00003B/4/P